Federated Identity Primer

Federated Identity Primer

Derrick Rountree

ELSEVIER

AMSTERDAM • BOSTON • HEIDELBERG • LONDON
NEW YORK • OXFORD • PARIS • SAN DIEGO
SAN FRANCISCO • SINGAPORE • SYDNEY • TOKYO
Syngress is an imprint of Elsevier

SYNGRESS.

Syngress is an imprint of Elsevier
The Boulevard, Langford Lane, Kidlington, Oxford, OX5 1GB, UK
225 Wyman Street, Waltham, MA 02451, USA

First published 2013

Notices
Knowledge and best practice in this field are constantly changing. As new research and
experience broaden our understanding, changes in research methods, professional practices, or
medical treatment may become necessary.

Practitioners and researchers must always rely on their own experience and knowledge in
evaluating and using any information, methods, compounds, or experiments described herein.
In using such information or methods they should be mindful of their own safety and the safety
of others, including parties for whom they have a professional responsibility.

To the fullest extent of the law, neither the Publisher nor the authors, contributors, or editors,
assume any liability for any injury and/or damage to persons or property as a matter of products
liability, negligence or otherwise, or from any use or operation of any methods, products,
instructions, or ideas contained in the material herein.

British Library Cataloguing in Publication Data
A catalogue record for this book is available from the British Library

Library of Congress Cataloging-in-Publication Data
A catalog record for this book is available from the Library of Congress

ISBN: 978-0-12-407189-6

For information on all Syngress publications
visit our website at store.elsevier.com

This book has been manufactured using Print On Demand technology. Each copy is produced
to order and is limited to black ink. The online version of this book will show color figures where
appropriate.

CONTENTS

PREFACE

The concept of federated identity is nothing new. In fact, it has been around a long time. It just never really caught on, partially because its usage scenarios were limited. But, that has changed. Now with the increased usage of cloud and Internet-based applications, federated identity has started to gain a lot of traction. Instances of federated identity are popping up all over the IT landscape. Not only is it being used on the Internet, but it is also being used within enterprises and other organizations. If you haven't come across an instance of federated identity yet, you most likely will in the very near future.

WHAT TO EXPECT FROM THIS BOOK

The purpose of this book is to provide you with a general introduction to federated identity. We will talk about federated identity and the technologies used to implement it. We will not discuss actual implementation details, but we will cover all the basics you need to know in order to get started using and implementing federated identity.

We will start in Chapter 1 by going over the concept of identity. Identity can mean a lot of things. We'll briefly cover physical identity just to give you a little background. Then we'll get into digital identity. We'll go over what your digital identity can be used for and why it should be protected. Finally, in this chapter we will introduce what I call the Internet Identity Problem. We'll talk about the problem and how federated identity can be used to solve it.

In Chapter 2, we'll start by giving a little background info and common terminology used when talking about identity management and federated identity. We will give some background on authentication, authorization, and access control. Understanding these concepts helps lay the foundation for understanding how federated identity is established and implemented. Then, we will start talking about federated identity and why you would want to use it.

In Chapter 3, we will dive into technology. There are many different methods for implementing federated identity. But, most of these methods share common technologies and protocols. This chapter will go over some of those common technologies and protocols. Once you have a good understanding of these technologies, it will make it a little easier for you to understand the different federated identity methodologies.

In Chapter 4, we will discuss some of the deployment options. There are cloud-based deployment options and on-premise options. We'll talk about some of the things you should consider when making your decision regarding which solution to use. We will also cover two of the more commonly used solutions: ADFS 2.0 and Access Control Services.

CHAPTER 1

Introduction to Identity

Information in this chapter:

- What Is Identity?
- The Internet Identity Problem

1.1 INTRODUCTION

Before we get into federated identity, let's just talk for a minute about identity itself. After all, if you don't understand identity, how can you understand federated identity? Identity may seem like a straightforward concept, but it's actually a little more complicated than people think. What makes it so complicated is the fact that someone's overall identity encompasses a lot more factors than you might first think. My goal in this chapter is to make sure you have a good understanding of what these factors are and how they come into play. Once you understand the overall concept of identity, then we will talk about what I call *the Internet identity problem*. The Internet identity problem is probably why you bought this book in the first place. You are being faced with the problem, and you are hoping that federated identity is the answer.

When breaking down the concepts, it becomes apparent that we cannot fully understand federated identity until we understand identity itself. This is why this chapter is so important. So, you need to make sure that you have a good understanding of the information in this chapter before you move onto the next one. It will make the subsequent concepts a lot easier to understand.

1.2 WHAT IS IDENTITY?

To put it succinctly, your identity is the set of characteristics that make you who you are. To understand the concept a little easier, we will break your identity up into two categories: your physical identity and your digital identity. This book focuses on what is considered digital identity. But, before we can talk about that, we'll quickly review physical identity so we can draw analogies between physical and digital identity concepts throughout the remainder of this text. Once we paint a clear picture of what physical identity is, its main characteristics, and how it is used, we will relate them to their digital equivalents. Although physical identity and digital identity refer to two different things, the fundamental concepts are the same. Getting a good grasp on the concept of physical identity will help you get a better grasp on the concept of digital identity much more quickly.

1.2.1 Physical Identity

When related to our daily lives, your physical identity is what identifies you as a person. It consists of many different factors and is not limited to your name and mailing address. In fact, it's much more. It encompasses everything about you: your physical characteristics, your personality, and your day-to-day behavior.

The characteristics of your physical identity can be used to help differentiate you from others. There are no two people that share all of the same physical identity characteristics. There may be two people who are close, but they're not exactly the same. Even in the case of identical twins, they are identical in many ways, but there are still distinguishing characteristics that can be used to tell them apart. You just have to know what characteristics to look for.

1.2.1.1 Components of Your Physical Identity

Describing your physical identity is not as simple as we may think. There's a lot more to it than what readily comes to mind. Let's try to break it down. For starters, there are three main components that make up your physical identity: your physical characteristics, your behavior and personality, and your personal information. In this section, we will cover each of these components in more detail.

Let's start with some of the more notable pieces of your physical identity, your physical characteristics. Your body's physical characteristics are the easiest pieces of your identity to identify. Your body's physical characteristics play a huge role in identifying who you are. In fact, when someone doesn't know a person's name or other personal information, they will generally use physical characteristics to identify that individual. Physical characteristics include height, build, age, hair color, complexion, etc.

Physical characteristics can be a very effective way of identifying someone. Often physical characteristics are the only information about a person that you may have available to you. As an example, let's say you witnessed a crime being committed. As a witness, you will most likely be questioned by the police. Assuming you do not personally know the individual who committed the crime, the police will ask you for a physical description of the assailant. Your description of the assailant's physical characteristics is a big part of what the police will use to track down the suspect.

In addition to the more frequently considered physical characteristics, there are others that aren't usually readily thought of. The way you walk, the way you talk, and the way you laugh are also parts of your physical characteristics; even though these characteristics are usually less noticed by most people. For instance, everyone has a distinctive voice. Even though the differences may not be apparent to the untrained ear, with the right equipment, it is possible to differentiate someone's voice from anyone else's.

One key point here is that physical characteristics are usually available to be viewed by basically anyone. Anyone who can see you or anyone that comes into close proximity with you can identify some of your physical characteristics. They don't require any special knowledge. They don't have to know you or request your permission to view these characteristics. They are just openly available to them. In addition, unless you live in a bubble, you can't prevent someone from seeing these physical characteristics.

The next set of physical identity characteristics consist of your behavior and what could be considered your personality. This includes your likes and your dislikes, the way you act in different situations and the attitude you display toward events in your life. For example, take your likes and dislikes. Some people like vegetables; others like me, don't like them. This is just one way I may be different from someone else. Then there is your reaction to certain situations. Some people sweat when they get nervous, others feel queasy. Some people don't react at all. Each person is different.

Each person has their own preferences. They behave differently in different situations. One thing to notice here is that, like your physical characteristics, your behavior and personality are something people can observe. They might not be able to figure everything out right away. They may have to observe you over a period of time, but it's definitely possible to figure out a person's behavior patterns.

This brings us to the final set of physical characteristics, your personal information. There is one very big difference between your personal information and the other physical identity characteristics we talked about. Your personal information cannot simply be observed. Usually this kind of information has to be offered by the person or someone familiar with the person. Some of these characteristics include your name, your address, and your social security number. It's very hard to figure out someone's name or address without conducting some sort of research, even if it's a simple online address lookup. Because of the confidentiality of this type of information, most people will not readily know this type of information about you, nor will they be able to obtain it from observation alone.

1.2.1.2 Protecting Your Physical Identity

Whenever you meet someone for the first time or fill out some sort of application, you will start by giving your name. Your name is probably your main piece of identification. Then, depending on the circumstances or context, you may need to provide more information like your address or social security number. People are generally somewhat restrictive when disclosing their address and should be very restrictive when disclosing their social security number. Before disclosing private information such as social security number, an initial screening (of varying depth) typically occurs in order to establish trust: the requestor will generally have to identify themselves and be verified as someone who is trustworthy.

This concept is more important than you might think. If we freely offer private information without verification, we put ourselves at risk, such as identity theft and fraud. Therefore, we must protect our identity. Trust plays a big part in the identity arena. We will see that the issue of trust will come up again and again as we progress through this book.

Why is trust so important? It's important because your identity furnishes you with access to resources available only to you. You use your identity to cash checks, get credit cards, and apply for loans. If someone else were to get a hold of your identity information, they

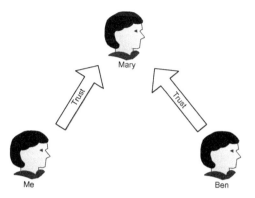

Fig. 1.1. Trusted friend.

could do all of these things in your name, without your permission and without your knowledge. Therefore, we need to ensure that only authorized individuals have access to our identity information.

There are several techniques that can be used to establish the trust needed (trustworthiness) before you can share your identity information with others. First, you could ask a person to show some sort of identification. This could be a driver's license, a passport, or some other sort of ID card. There is always the possibility of the driver's license or identification card being counterfeit. But, other than that, an ID card can give you some sense of comfort that a person is who they say they are.

Another way is to establish trust by using a third party. Both you and the person that you are trying to identify would have to know and trust this third party. If you trust the third party, then you can trust identifications that they make. For example, I know Mary, and Mary knows Ben. If I trust Mary, then I can believe her when she tells me who Ben is. I don't need to have personal knowledge of Ben beforehand (Fig. 1.1).

Sometimes there will be situations where you won't have friends in common or know the same person but you may be separated by two or more people. In this case, you trust someone that trusts someone who knows the other person. It's not as complicated as it sounds. It's like "a friend of a friend" tells you who someone is. This will more than likely be the more common scenario. With the large number of people that exist in the world, it's impossible for you to have a single friend in common with everyone (Fig. 1.2).

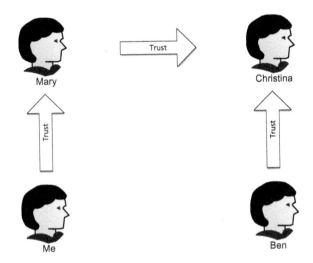

Fig. 1.2. Friend of a friend.

1.2.1.3 Only One Physical Identity

Because your physical identity theoretically encompasses everything about you, it's safe to say that everyone only has one physical identity. For example, most people only have one personality. You may act differently in different situations, but you still only have one personality and the different behaviors are part of the same personality.

Depending on the situation, certain aspects of your physical identity are more relevant than others. All aspects together make up your identity, but they are not all relevant to all situations. Generally, most people will only care about a subset of someone's physical identity characteristics. That doesn't mean that the other characteristics aren't important, it just means they aren't needed to identify you to a particular person. For example, unless you work at a circus, I'm sure your employer doesn't care whether you are afraid of clowns. But, your husband or wife would probably care. Pieces of your identity don't just go away because someone doesn't care about those parts. They're still a part of you; they just may not be relevant to a particular situation.

1.2.2 Digital Identity

Now that we have talked about physical identity, it's time for use to move into digital identity. First, I would just like to point out that from this point on, when we talk about identity, unless specifically stated otherwise, we are referring to your digital identity. Your digital identity is what identifies you in the digital world, or what some would call the computer world. This is a relatively new concept.

Originally people just simply did whatever they wanted on a computer, and nothing was tracked. This has changed dramatically over the years. The changes themselves didn't happen rapidly, they happened over time. But, if you look at where we're at and compare it to where we started, there is definitely a big difference.

First web sites started tracking activities. Web sites would track information about their visitors. They would track user preferences and selections. That way the user wouldn't have to make the same selections and set the same preferences every time they visited a site. Their settings would be saved and the web site would display however they wanted it, based on those settings. In general, this was done through the use of browser cookies. Cookies are used to store user-specific information about a particular web site. Cookies are great, but, in general, the information inside a cookie could only be accessed by the site that created it, so all information was tracked individually (on a site-by-site basis).

The next step in the evolution was for web sites to start sharing information with each other. When information is shared, your first visit to a web site can be customized just for you. A lot of sites use this shared information to create customized advertising just for you. To make this possible, information is not just collected by web sites. Instead, search engines and web browsers collect and store your information so it is readily available to the various web sites you visit.

The digital world kept evolving. Nowadays, computers aren't the only devices used to access the Internet. You can use smartphones, tablets, and a host of other devices. Almost everything you do in the digital world is tracked, and in most cases, the information is correlated with other information and shared with almost anyone who wants it and is willing to pay for it. This information is used to build a digital profile for you. This profile forms the beginnings of a digital identity. Your full digital profile also includes more detailed information.

1.2.2.1 Components of Your Digital Identity

Similar to your physical identity, your digital identity is not just something simple like your username. It's composed of all the information that makes you who you are in the digital world. There are many components that make up your digital identity including your user account, your digital behavior, your personal information, and even various components of your physical identity.

Usually when people think about digital identity, they think about a user account. And when they think about a user account, they only think about a username (or user ID). Your user account can contain much more information than just a username. There are some fairly obvious components like your full name and your membership status. But, there are other less common components like your location and your phone number. Looking at Fig. 1.3, you can see the multitude of attributes that can be associated with a user account.

When you use the Internet there are certain digital characteristics associated with your access. You can think of these characteristics as being analogous to the physical characteristics associated with your physical identity. Most of the characteristics are easily determined by the web site or system you are accessing. Some of these characteristics

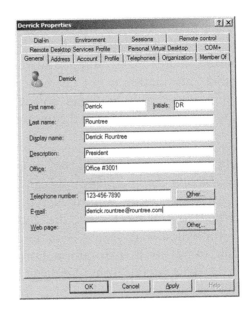

Fig. 1.3. User account properties.

include your IP address, the web browser you are using to access the web site, and the operating system or device you are using.

Similar to your physical identity, your digital identity includes your behavior but in this case it is your behavior in the digital world: the sites you visit, when you last logged in, the systems you use, etc. In most cases, no two people will visit the same site at the same time, using the same device. This is why your digital behavior can be used as a differentiating factor.

In fact, paying attention to a person's digital behavior has led to a new form of authentication called risk-based authentication. In risk-based authentication, a risk score is calculated based on whether or not the current user is performing digital actions he or she usually performs. This risk score is used to determine whether or not the user will be allowed to log in.

Your digital identity can also include certain aspects of your physical identity. For example, biometrics are sometimes used as a means of authentication. In the case of biometrics, your fingerprints, your retina, or iris can all be included as part of your digital identity. Samples of certain physical characteristics are taken and stored in a user profile. This user profile is part of your digital identity, which is verified by comparing your sample at the time of login to the sample stored in your user profile.

In the digital world, there is a lot of information about you that would be considered somewhat personal. Items like your username, e-mail address, and credit card numbers. Some of this information you may give up freely, like your e-mail address, but you may think twice before sharing your credit card number. In order for you to feel comfortable submitting your credit card information to a web site, you'd probably want to first make sure that the site can be trusted.

1.2.2.2 Protecting Your Digital Identity

Just like your physical identity needs to be protected, so does your digital identity. In the digital world, there is information you might freely share, such as your e-mail address. But there is other information you shouldn't provide unless the recipient—in this case the system receiving the information—has been identified. Giving information to the wrong person or system can have very profound effects on your life. Similar to the loss of your physical identity information, losing your digital identity information can put you at risk of identity theft and fraud, so it's important that you take the necessary steps to prevent your digital identity from being leaked.

One way to validate this identity is for the system to obtain a digital certificate. If a system or web site has been identified using a digital certificate, then you might be more comfortable submitting your credit card information. We will cover digital certificates in more detail in Chapter 2 but for now, know that the digital certificate specifies the name of the web site to which it was issued. The certificate was issued by a trusted authority, therefore, you trust that the information contained within the certificate is true.

1.2.2.3 Only One Digital Identity

Just like with your physical identity, you only have one digital identity. Not all web sites that you visit will care about all of your identity information. In fact, most sites will only request a small portion of your identity information. Any information that was not requested will be discarded if it is sent to the site. For example, if a web site doesn't use your IP address in any processing, it will not request it even though that information is readily available.

1.3 THE INTERNET IDENTITY PROBLEM

Before we can propose federated identity as a solution, we must first clarify the problem we're trying to solve. With the coming of the "cloud era," there has been a proliferation of web-based applications. This has been a great help for companies looking to decrease their internal IT footprint but it has brought about a problem. When applications were mostly internal, administrators could configure them to support a single set of credentials. However, most providers of Internet-based services store user credentials in different places; in most cases in their own directory store or database, which are not shared with other providers. This results in users having multiple sets of credentials. In most cases, a user will have a different set of credentials for each provider.

Having to remember all of these credentials is not only cumbersome for the user. It also causes other issues. For example, each set of credentials has its own user and password policies, which may differ from the internal corporate polices.

There have been multiple attempts to solve this problem. Providers have come up with ways to allow single sign on. Some providers allow you to create custom keys or tokens to use for login. These tokens are created based on a set of credentials that the user already has. Problems with these methods are that they are proprietary and they must be reconfigured for each new application that is brought online, at potentially great cost. Therefore, these methods do not scale very well. Other proposed solutions have similar drawbacks.

Federated identity was built to address these authentication issues. Based on standards that can be applied to any environment, the federated identity architecture is designed to allow for scaling to support a very large number of environments. In the following chapters, we will expand on federated identity and how it can be used to solve the authentication problem.

1.4 SUMMARY

Although your physical identity and your digital identity are different, the concepts are the same. Your physical identity includes your physical characteristics, your behavior, and your personal information. Your digital identity includes your digital characteristics, your digital behavior, pieces of your physical identity, and your personal information. Both your physical and your digital identities need to be protected. You need to ensure that you are not providing your information to people, systems, or web sites that cannot be trusted.

More and more people and organizations are facing the same problems when it comes to digital identities. In a world, where more and more applications and services are being offered by different service providers, there needs to be a better way for your digital identity to follow you. This is where federated identity comes in. Your identity is stored in one place and your information can be sent to applications and services that need it.

CHAPTER 2

What Is Federated Identity?

Information in this chapter:

- Authentication and Authorization
- Access Control
- Federated Service Model
- Federated Identity

2.1 INTRODUCTION

Now that we have established a solid understanding of identity, it's time to discuss federated identity. We will cover the definition of federated identity and why you would want to use it.

Federated identity is actually a combination of different components and concepts that come together to form one solution. The components of the solution are just as important as the solution itself, so this is where we will start. We will cover authentication and authorization, access control, and the identity provider (IdP)/service provider model individually before we put them together to form a federated identity solution.

2.2 AUTHENTICATION AND AUTHORIZATION

The concepts of authentication and authorization are at the core of federated identity. One of the key problems people have when studying authentication and authorization is understanding the difference between the two. Many times, authentication and authorization are just grouped together and considered one concept for practical or implementation purposes. However, when it comes to federated identity knowing the difference is very important. In fact, federated identity is based on the fact that the two concepts are not the same. In this section, we review authentication and authorization and the differences between the two.

2.2.1 Authentication

Authentication is the process of verifying that you are who you say you are. Whenever sensitive information is involved or auditing needs to be performed, it is important to validate that the person performing an action is who they say they are. Otherwise, the information they provide cannot be trusted. This is why, before you can access resources on most systems, you have to prove your identity or authenticate yourself.

Authentication is broken down into two components: identification and verification. Identification occurs before verification. Identification is the process of stating who you are. This statement could be in the form of a username, an e-mail address, or some other method that identifies you. Basically, you are saying, I am drountree or I am derrick@gmail.com; and I want access to the resources that are available to me.

But, how does the system know that you really are drountree? The system can't just give access to anyone who claims to be drountree. This is where verification comes in. Verification is the process that a system goes through to check that you are indeed who you say you are. This is what most people think of when they think of authentication. They don't realize that the first part of the process is establishing your identity. Verification can be performed in many ways. You supply a password, a Personal Identification Number (PIN), or use some type of biometric identifier.

Think about it this way. You know that when you attempt to authenticate to a system and you enter your username and password, the system will check to see that the combination you have entered is correct. A correct combination of the two is needed for successful authentication. You need to enter the password that corresponds to the username you provided. If one or the other is wrong, then the authentication attempt will fail. The system first checks to see that the username you entered is valid. If it isn't, an error will be immediately returned. If it is valid, then the password will be checked. If the password is correct, then the authentication attempt will be successful.

2.2.1.1 Types of Authentication

There are many types of authentication available. For the purpose of understanding federated authentication, it's not important that you have an in-depth understanding of all types of authentication but, it is a good idea to have a general understanding of what they are. As you will see later on, federated identity solutions support a wide variety of authentication methods. So when you are looking at setting up a federated identity solution, you will have to make a decision about which authentication methods you want to use; so we will go over some of the more common methods of authentication in use today.

2.2.1.1.1 Username and Password

This is the simplest and most commonly used method of authentication. I feel like I need to get a little deep into this one; just to clear up some misconceptions. First let's get this out of the way. *Username and password* is not really a type of authentication. Many people refer to it as such, but it's not. It's simply a format you may use to supply your credentials. Your credentials themselves could then be processed in a number of different ways. These different ways are the actual authentication methods. The backend systems could be using NT LAN Manager (NTLM), Challenge-Handshake Authentication Protocol (CHAP), or a multitude of other authentication mechanisms; so if you run into a vendor that uses username and password for authentication, you might want to check the actual authentication mechanism being used. It may or may not be very secure. As an additional security precaution, you should also check how the credentials are stored.

2.2.1.1.2 Biometrics

Biometric authentication involves using some part of your physical makeup to authenticate you. This could be a fingerprint, an iris scan, a retina scan, or some other physical characteristic. A single characteristic or multiple characteristics could be used. It all depends on the infrastructure and the level of security desired. With biometric authentication, the physical characteristic being examined is usually mapped to a username. This username is used to make decisions after the person has been authenticated. In some cases, the user must enter the username when attempting to authenticate; in others, a lookup is done on the biometric sample in order to determine the username.

Biometric authentication is performed by doing a comparison of the physical aspect you present for authentication against a copy that has been stored. For example, you would place your finger on a fingerprint reader for comparison against the stored sample. If your fingerprint matches the stored sample, then the authentication is considered to be successful.

In order to set up biometric authentication the appropriate infrastructure must be in place. Once the infrastructure is set up we register users. Some products allow users to register directly while others require a registration agent to perform the registration for the user. Let's take the example of fingerprint-based authentication. During the registration process, the system will ask the user to submit a sample, in actual fact it will create multiple samples. The user places their finger on the fingerprint reader. The system will record images of the user's fingerprint. The system will use the multiple images to determine a point pattern to identify the user's fingerprint. These points are basically dots placed on different areas of the fingerprint. These dots are used to denote the pattern made by the fingerprint. Once a sufficient number of samples have been taken to form a consistent point pattern, the pattern is stored and used as the basis for later comparison during authentication.

Biometric authentication is a fairly solid method of authentication and is in use by many organizations today but, it is not without its issues or drawbacks. One of the problems with biometric authentication is that it usually requires special hardware such as a fingerprint reader, retina scanner, and so on. The hardware has to be installed and configured on each system (or endpoint) that will be used for login. This limits the overall usability of the solution. You can't just walk up to any system and expect to use it to authenticate. It can be especially problematic when you are external to your organization (i.e., working remotely or on the road), as you need a system that has the necessary hardware installed and configured per the corporate policy. In addition, cost can also be an issue with biometrics. The specialized hardware required for biometric authentication can be expensive and has to be purchased for all authentication endpoints. Therefore, the initial investment required for a biometric solution can be quite sizeable.

A second potential concern with biometrics is security. Part of setting up a biometric solution includes configuring the sensitivity level for the sample. The sensitivity level determines how close a match you need for authentication to be successful. Configuring the sensitivity level can be somewhat tricky. If it's set too low, one recorded sample could potentially match multiple physical samples. If it's set too high, you could block access to someone who is legitimately authorized to access the system.

There have also been cases where people have been able to break biometric authentication. The main issue here is that in many cases, biometric authentication relies only on the image presented during authentication, so it can be tricked by a forged image (we see plenty of examples of this in modern-day spy films). In order to combat this, some biometric manufacturers have been adding other requirements to their biometric authentication solution. For example, a fingerprint reader may also check the temperature of the finger used to supply the fingerprint. If the temperature is not within a normal range for the human body, the system assumes the fingerprint is being supplied by some bogus method and the authentication fails.

For these reasons, we do not see a lot of Internet-based applications using biometric authentication. We see it more in corporate settings and, many times, it's used just for certain applications or under special circumstances.

2.2.1.1.3 User Certificates

Digital certificates can also be used to authenticate users. Digital certificates contain a unique key pair that is associated with the certificate. This is how certificates can be differentiated from one another. There is a certain type of digital certificate called a user certificate that is specifically designed for user authentication. After the certificate is created, the certificate is then mapped back to a user account. This user account is used to determine what access the user should have. When the user attempts to access a resource, a certificate will be requested. Depending on the client device and server configuration, a user certificate may automatically be submitted or the user may have to specify which certificate to submit. The certificate is accepted by the resource and processed. During the processing, the backend authentication system will look up the certificate and find the corresponding user account for that certificate. This information is then submitted to the resource. The resource will then make authorization decisions based on the user account.

In order to use certificate-based authentication, the certificate must be somehow stored and transported. There are a few options. One option is to have the operating system on your computer storing the certificate. The problem with this is that the certificate is not portable. You can only use it from that system. Another, more popular alternative is to use a smartcard. A smartcard uses integrated circuits to store the digital certificate. When you attempt to access a resource and the site requests a certificate, you type in your PIN to unlock your smartcard and the certificate is submitted to the resource. Smartcards also have a portability issue. They require specialized hardware (smartcard readers) to be attached to computer systems to enable and allow the systems to retrieve information from the smartcards. The need for this personalized hardware is the reason smartcards haven't taken off for Internet application authentication, compared to their adoption at the enterprise level.

2.2.1.1.4 Kerberos

Kerberos is a ticketing-based authentication system, based on the use of symmetric keys. Kerberos uses tickets to provide authentication to resources instead of passwords. This eliminates the threat of password stealing via network sniffing. One of the biggest benefits of Kerberos is its ability to provide single sign-on (SSO). Once you log into your Kerberos environment, you will be automatically logged into other applications in the environment.

To help provide a secure environment, Kerberos makes use of Mutual Authentication. In Mutual Authentication, both the server and the client must be authenticated. The client knows that the server can be trusted, and the server knows that the client can be trusted. This authentication helps prevent man-in-the-middle attacks and spoofing. Kerberos is also time sensitive. The tickets in a Kerberos environment must be renewed periodically or they will expire.

The key components in a Kerberos system are the Key Distribution Center (KDC), the Authentication Service, and the Ticket Granting Service.

- *Key Distribution Center*—KDC is the center of the Kerberos process. The KDC holds a database of the keys used in the authentication process and consists of two main parts: an Authentication Service and a Ticket Granting Service.
- *Authentication Service*—The Authentication Service authenticates the client.
- *Ticket Granting Service*—The Ticket Granting Service provides tickets and Ticket Granting Tickets to the client systems. Ticket Granting Tickets contain the client ID, the client network address, the ticket validity period, and the Ticket Granting Server session key.

The following points outline the Kerberos authentication process as shown in Fig. 2.1:

1. The user enters a username and password at the client system.
2. The client uses a one-way hash to mask the password. This one-way hash is considered the client secret.
3. The client sends the username to the Authentication Server.
4. The Authentication Server retrieves the user password from the credential store and creates a one-way hash.
5. The Authentication Server checks to ensure that the client is in the approved client database.
6. If the client is approved, the Authentication Server will send back a Ticket Granting Server session key and a Ticket Granting Ticket.
7. The client is then authenticated to the Ticket Granting Server.

The following points outline the Kerberos resource request process as shown in Fig. 2.2:

1. The client sends a request to the Ticket Granting Service. The request contains the Ticket Granting Ticket and an authenticator encrypted using the Ticket Granting Server session key.

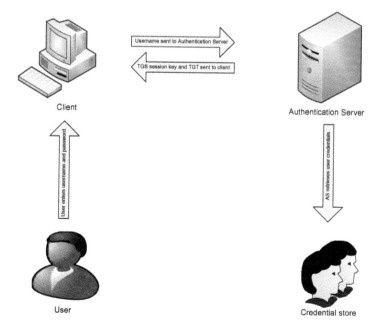

Fig. 2.1. Kerberos authentication flow.

2. The Ticket Granting Service sends the client a client-to-server ticket and a client/server session key.
3. The client sends the client-to-server ticket and a new authenticator to the server where the resource resides.
4. The server then sends a confirmation message back to the client.
5. The client confirms the server and begins sending requests.

Kerberos is commonly used in corporate environments or within an organization. One of the problems with Kerberos is that the systems have to belong to the same realm. A realm is a logical security grouping. A system's realm is established using client software on the system. As you may have guessed, the issue here is that systems running Internet-based applications generally do not reside in the same realm as the clients that access them. Therefore, Kerberos cannot be used in these situations.

There are some service providers that offer Kerberos services for Internet-based applications to alleviate this problem but these implementations are still in the early stages and typically require software to

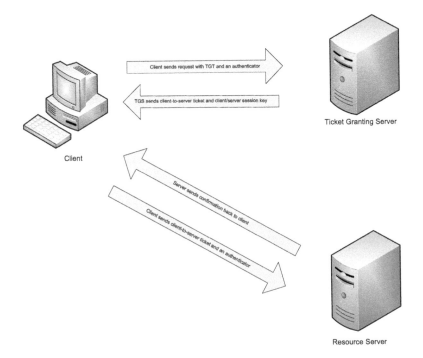

Fig. 2.2. Kerberos resource access.

be installed on the client system. Having to install client software on the end user system can be a deterrent for Internet application users.

2.2.1.1.5 One-Time-Use Token

One-time-use tokens present the user with an alphanumeric code that must be entered into the authentication system. The codes can be generated multiple ways and made available via a hardware device, like a key fob (usually called hard tokens) or through an application installed on the client system (usually called soft tokens).

The hardware device or application that generates the tokens is tied to a particular user so only that user can authenticate using the codes provided by the key fob or application. In order to use a one-time-use token for authentication, the user must enter their username and token code. The token codes are synchronized with the authentication server. Once the user enters the username and token, these are submitted for authentication. The username and code are compared against those on the authentication server. If they match, then authentication is successful.

For security reasons, the token codes generated by token devices generally are time sensitive. This means the code will change after a given interval. In most cases, once a code is used to authenticate it cannot be used again. You have to wait until a new code is generated before you can authenticate again.

One-time-use token implementations can be expensive because of the costs associated with purchasing key fobs and soft tokens, as well as the infrastructure to support them. There are also administration and maintenance costs associated with registering users, distributing hard tokens, and installing the soft tokens.

2.2.1.1.6 Risk-Based Authentication

Risk-based authentication is a fairly new concept. It's being used on an increasing number of web sites; especially sites where security is paramount, like financial services. Risk-based authentication is based on the calculation of a risk score. If the risk is too high, access is not permitted. To calculate the risk score, user behavior is examined. Some of the factors checked are sites visited, device and browser used to access the site, and what time the user usually visits the site. Depending on how many of these factors match the usual client behavior, the score may be such that authentication will be denied.

Many risk-based authentication mechanisms require a client to be installed on the end-user device to gather and track the information used to calculate the risk. In some cases, this is too intrusive to be used.

2.2.1.1.7 Custom Authentication Tokens

Many sites often use custom tokens for authentication. These tokens are usually manifested in the form of a cookie. These custom tokens are used for the purpose of SSO. The user starts by authenticating to one site. After successful authentication, a cookie is created. This cookie is used to authenticate the user to other sites.

This method can be a convenient way to achieve SSO to most sites. But, there are definitely drawbacks. The biggest of which is the fact that the solution is not portable. It's not easily moved from one site to another. In fact, what usually happens is that you have to create a different token for each site you want to sign into. In addition, because the solution is not based on any standard, a change to one of the sites involved in the process may require a complete rework of the solution. As you may have guessed, costs can quickly build up when using this type of solution, which is why many organizations try to avoid it when possible.

2.2.1.2 Other Authentication Concepts

Authentication isn't just about the different types of authentication available. Before we close out authentication, there are a couple of other authentication concepts that you should be aware of. We are going to talk about mutual authentication and multifactor authentication. These two concepts are used as part of or in conjunction with the different authentication types we've already covered.

2.2.1.2.1 Mutual Authentication

Generally, in an authentication system, the client must be authenticated before it is allowed to access the server. But what about the server? How can the client be sure that the server is who it says it is? If the server's identity is not verified, then it's possible the server could be falsified; then the client could be submitting credentials to a malicious entity. This is where mutual authentication comes in.

In mutual authentication, not only is the client authenticated, but the server is also authenticated. The server must do something to prove its identity. This could be in the form of a server certificate or some sort of private key. Once the server has been authenticated and the client trusts the server, then the client will send its credentials to the server. This provides for a more secure authentication process and a more secure environment overall.

2.2.1.2.2 Multifactor Authentication

Multifactor authentication gets its name from the use of multiple authentication factors. So what is an authentication factor? You can think of a factor as a category of authentication. There are three authentication factors that can be used: something you know, something you have, and something you are. Something you know would be a password, a PIN, or some other personal information. Something you have would be a one-time-use token, a smartcard, or some other artifact that you might have in your physical possession. Something you are would be your biometric identity like a fingerprint or a speech pattern. In order for something to be considered multifactor authentication, it must make use of at least two of the three factors mentioned.

People often confuse two-factor authentication with dual authentication. Dual authentication is basically using any two forms of authentication in conjunction. For dual authentication, it doesn't matter if these two forms of authentication are from the same factor or not. For example, requiring two passwords would be dual authentication, but it would not be considered two-factor authentication. In order for authentication to be truly two-factor, you must use authentication methods that are classified in two different factors.

Multifactor authentication is often used in situations where more stringent security is required. For example, you may require multifactor authentication when using a Virtual Private Network (VPN) to access your organization's internal network. In cases like these, you want to take extra precautions to ensure the right person is accessing the network.

2.2.2 Authorization

After users have been identified and verified using authentication, then comes authorization. Authorization is the process of specifying what a user is allowed to do. Authorization is more than just a system concept. Authorization effects take place everywhere in your organization. Your organization should have a security policy that defines the authorization within your entire organization. The policy should specify who is allowed to access which resources and what they are allowed to do with these resources.

After you have finalized your authorization policy, then it's time to configure your systems to reflect the decisions outlined in your policy. In some cases, you have to authenticate to the system making the authorization decisions. In other cases you don't. It just depends on the system and what method the system is using to make the authorization decisions. Some common examples are username, e-mail address, and group membership.

2.3 ACCESS CONTROL

Once you have defined your authentication and authorization policies, an access control system is what you would use to enforce them. Access control systems are used to enforce permissions on systems and resources. There are three main access control models used today: Mandatory Access Control (MAC), Discretionary Access Control (DAC), and Role-Based Access Control (RBAC). Some organizations use only one model; but some use multiple models. Each has its own advantages and disadvantages.

2.3.1 Mandatory Access Control

MAC is based on a hierarchical model. The hierarchy is based on security level. All users are assigned a security or clearance level. All objects are assigned a security label. Users can only access resources that correspond to a security level equal to or lower than theirs in the hierarchy.

In a MAC model, access is controlled strictly by the administrator. The administrator sets all permissions. Users cannot set their own permissions, even if they own the object. Because of this, MAC systems are considered very secure. This is because of the centralized administration. Centralized administration makes it easier for the administrator to control who has access to what. The administrator doesn't have to worry about someone else setting permissions improperly. Because of the high-level security in MAC systems, MAC access models are often used in government systems.

There are some disadvantages to MAC systems. MAC systems can be quite cumbersome to manage. This is because the administrator must assign all permissions. Therefore, the administrator assumes the entire burden for configuration and maintenance. An administrator can quickly become overwhelmed as the systems grow larger and more complex. You must ensure that your administrative staff is resourced properly to handle the load. This is one of the main reasons MAC systems are generally not used in Internet-based applications. The large user population would be very difficult to manage.

2.3.2 Discretionary Access Control

DAC is based on Access Control Lists (ACLs). The ACL lists which users have access to an object and what they can do with that object. The ACL lists users and permissions. You specifically grant or deny permissions.

MAC systems use a more distributed administrative architecture. In a MAC model, access is determined by the object owner. So if you are the owner of an object, you have full control in determining who else can access that object.

Most PC operating systems use a MAC model. Figure 2.3 shows an example from a Windows 8 system. You can see the ACL for one of the folders on the system.

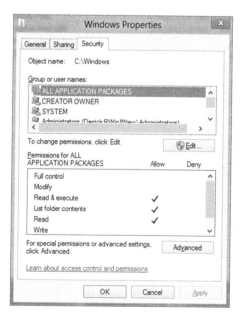

Fig. 2.3. Windows 8 folder permissions window.

DAC systems are generally easier to manage than MAC systems. The distrusted administrative model puts less of a burden on the administrator. The administrator is not responsible for setting the permissions for every system.

DAC systems can be a little less secure than MAC systems. This is in part due the distributed management model. Since the administrator does not control all object access, it's possible that permissions could be set incorrectly, potentially leading to a breach of information. The administrator can get around this by setting up a group of systems that will only be managed by the administrator. These systems can be used to store more sensitive information.

2.3.3 Role-Based Access Control

RBAC systems are based on a user's roles and responsibilities. Users aren't given access to systems, roles are assigned to users, and access is granted to roles. In an RBAC system, roles are centrally managed by the administrator. The administrator determines what roles exist within their company and then maps these roles to job functions and tasks. Roles can effectively be implemented using security groups. You start by creating a security group representing each role and you assign permissions and rights to these groups. Then you simply add the appropriate users to the appropriate security groups, depending on their role or job function.

Since access is defined based on roles and specific job functions, you have more knowledge of what access users really require to perform this job. This aids in being able to grant access based on the principle of least privilege. The principle of least privilege states that users should be given the minimum amount of rights needed for them to do their job. Role-based access models also lend themselves to easier delegation. Delegation allows you to give administrative rights to someone else. You don't have to give them full administrative rights. You can specify certain rights for them or certain objects for them to have administrative rights over.

RBAC systems can be difficult to implement. This is in part due to the large amount of up-front work that must be done. A lot of effort is required to identify all the various roles within an organization. It's a little easier in a newer organization. But in a large, already-established organization it can take quite some time to identify all the necessary roles and configure your systems to recognize and make use of these roles.

Most Internet-based service providers use some sort of RBAC system. This makes it easier for them to automate user creation and access activities. Service providers have to deal with thousands and thousands of users. They can't spend much time figuring out what access each user needs so they just determine which role to place the user in and the user is automatically given the appropriate rights.

2.4 FEDERATED SERVICE MODEL

All the components we have talked about so far in this chapter come together to create a service model. A service model determines how users are authenticated and how services are delivered. The federated service model is the model used by federated identity solutions. The federated service model can be broken up into two required components: the IdP and the service provider. Without both of these components, you do not have a federated identity solution. Each of these components has distinct characteristics and responsibilities.

For everything to integrate properly there must be a trust relationship between the IdP and the service provider (or application). There are actually two trusts that are necessary. The IdP must trust the application or it will not send user information to the application. The application must trust the IdP or it will not trust the user identity information that comes from the IdP.

2.4.1 Identity Provider

An IdP is an entity that holds identity information. You can have an IdP set up internally, or you can use a service provider to provide identity services for you. Users, also called entities, will authenticate against the IdP's credential store. The IdP will then allow access to user's identity information. It's important to note that an IdP does more than just authenticate a user. It also holds the user's identity information. Upon authentication, this information can be sent to whichever trusted partner needs it.

2.4.1.1 Credential Store

The credential store, sometimes called the user store or the authentication store, is where the actual user credentials are stored. There are two main types of authentication stores being used with IdPs today: databases and directory stores. In general, with databases, credentials are stored in proprietary tables created by the user management application. One of the reasons databases are often chosen as credential stores is because a majority of developers have experience coding against a database, so it's relatively easy for them to create code to authenticate users against one. Directory stores include LDAP stores and Active Directory implementations. LDAP is the Lightweight Directory Access Protocol. It provides for a simple standards-based approach to accessing information from the credential store. Active Directory is Microsoft's domain-based approach to LDAP. Using an Active Directory credential store generally requires that you use approved proprietary access methods.

2.4.2 Service Provider

Service providers are the entities that provide services to others. These services could be applications, infrastructure, or data services. As "the cloud" grows in popularity, many people have become aware of the three main cloud services models. They are IaaS (Infrastructure as a Service), PaaS (Platform as a Service), and SaaS (Software as a Service). The applications and services provided by a service provider are called the relying party. This is because they rely on the IdP for authentication and identity information.

2.5 FEDERATED IDENTITY

Now that you have a little background on the technologies involved and how they're used, we can get into what exactly federated identity means. Federated identity means different things to different people. Usually, this happens because many people only understand a portion of the federated identity concept or what's needed to implement it.

One of the biggest confusions that exist around federated identity is how it is related to federated authentication. Therefore, first of all, you need to understand the difference between federated identity and federated authentication. Some people use the two terms interchangeably, but they are quite different. Federated authentication can be considered a subset of a federated identity solution. Your digital identity is basically who you are, what you do in the digital world, and other characteristics. As we've learned, authentication is basically just a way of verifying that you are who you say you are. Once you have verified you are who you say are, then your identity information can be unlocked. So, you can use federated authentication as a means to access federated identity information.

Federated authentication is the actual login process that takes place. You log into one place and that login allows you access somewhere else. What happens after that login is where other components of federated identity may or may not kick in. Federated authentication does not necessarily require an IdP to be in place. There may be some other systems in place where information is passed from one system to another. As I mentioned before, an IdP is necessary for you to have a true federated identity solution. So, what does this mean? This means that you can have federated authentication without federated identity.

Federated identity is a secure way for disparate systems to get access to your identity information. Your information may only exist in one system. But, with federated identity, other systems can also have access this information. The key to federated identity is trust. The system that holds your information and the system that is requesting your information must trust each other. The system that holds the information must trust the system that is requesting the information, in order to make sure your information is being transmitted to a trusted place. The system requesting the information has to trust the sender to ensure they are getting accurate and trustworthy information.

Basically, an application is trusting another entity, namely an IdP, when that entity says who a particular user is. The application does not perform any actions to verify the user's identity itself. It just believes what the IdP says. Before an application will believe an IdP, a trust relationship must be established. The application must be configured with the address of the IdP that it will be trusting. The IdP must be configured with the address of the application. In most cases, some type of keys will be exchanged between the two entities to actually establish the relationship. These keys are used by the entity to identify itself with the other entity.

2.5.1 Authentication vs Authorization with Federated Identity

One of the key characteristics of federated identity is that authentication is abstracted from authorization. So what does this mean? In most legacy applications, the application first authenticates the user. Then the application uses the response from the authentication request to make authorization decisions about what access and capabilities the

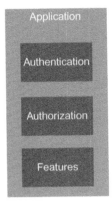

Fig. 2.4. Traditional authentication architecture.

user will have within the application. It should be noted, however, that just because the application performs the authentication, it doesn't mean the application actually does the authentication processing. The authentication could be done against Active Directory or some other system. They key is that the application itself is sending the authentication request.

With federated identity, the authentication request does not have to be performed by the application. Abstracting authentication from authorization means that the two processes can be done independently, even by different systems. You can use a third-party system, like an internal or external IdP to provide the authentication. The IdP sends the authentication information back to the application. The application then uses the information it received from the IdP to make authorization decisions and allow access to the user.

Figures 2.4 and 2.5 show the difference between a typical legacy application and a federated identity model. Figure 2.4 shows the typical legacy application. The user accesses the application. The application accesses the credential store directly to perform the authentication. The application will then use the authentication to make authorization decisions.

Figure 2.5 shows a federated authentication model. In the model, the concept of an IdP comes into play. The user accesses the application. The application talks to the IdP. Then the IdP talks to the credential store.

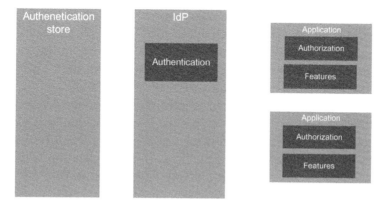

Fig. 2.5. Federated authentication architecture.

If you're still having trouble understanding, you can think of it like this. Let's say you and I have a mutual friend. One day that friend brings the two of us together. When he introduces me to you, he will tell you my name and maybe something about me. Although you and I have never met, you will believe the information given to you by our common friend because you trust that friend. In this scenario you are the application, I am the user, and the mutual friend is the IdP.

2.5.2 Federated Identity Advantages and Disadvantages

Federated identity, like anything else, has its advantages and disadvantages. Understanding these advantages and disadvantages will help you determine whether federated identity is right for your organization. Some would say implementing a federated identity solution is a "no brainer" but that's not the case. There are definitely distinct disadvantages to implementing federated identity. In addition, the advantages of federated identity don't really hold up in all scenarios so you should conduct a proper evaluation to ensure that it's right for your organization.

2.5.2.1 Advantages

Federated identity offers many advantages on the administration side and the user side. That's one of the beauties of federated identity. It's not just an admin feature or a user feature. It helps both sides. Many SSO solutions are good for the user but cause extra overhead for the administrator. These advantages include security, a seamless user experience, increased manageability, and extensibility.

2.5.2.1.1 Security of User Credentials

Many people worry about which applications they submit their credentials to. If the application is compromised, then an attacker would have access to the user's credentials. If you are using the same credentials with multiple applications this makes the dangers of someone compromising the password even greater. With federated identity solutions, the application itself never sees the user's credentials. The application only sees the identity information sent from the IdP. Only the IdP sees the user's credentials. Therefore, if the application is compromised you don't have to worry about anyone getting access to the users' credentials.

2.5.2.1.2 Seamless User Experience

Federated authentication is seamless to the user. In most cases, the end user will not realize that they are authenticating to a different system than the application they are trying to access. This seamlessness provides the benefits of federated authentication without negatively impacting the user experience.

2.5.2.1.3 Applications only Make Authorization Decisions

With federated authentication, applications are not responsible for authentication. They are only responsible for making authorization decisions. This helps to simplify application development. Authentications can be very complicated. Removing the need to code for authentication can really ease development efforts.

2.5.2.1.4 Reduce Account Management

Because federated identity abstracts authentication from authorization, users can be authenticated anywhere that is trusted by the application. Federated authentication allows you to use a third-party IdP for authentication. With a third-party IdP and authentication store you don't have to maintain accounts internally. This helps to ease your administrative burden.

2.5.2.1.5 Reduce Number of Usernames and Passwords

As we discussed before, most Internet-based applications use their own credential store. This causes users to have to remember multiple sets of credentials. When users have multiple sets of credentials, they will generally either use the same credentials or use easy-to-remember credentials. One of the big uses of federated identity and federated authentication is SSO. Once you log into your IdP, then that IdP can send your information to multiple applications. You don't have to log into these applications individually.

Switching to a federated identity solution will help reduce the number of credential sets that users need to memorize. Since there would be only one set of credentials that needs to be remembered, theoretically, users wouldn't mind using a complex set of credentials. This would help increase the overall security of users' applications.

In addition, the SSO provided by federated authentication is seen as very secure. One common method for SSO is credential storage. SSO systems that store credentials are seen as less secure because they are still passing passwords back and forth. Not to mention the fact that all your passwords are stored in one location, so that location has to be extremely secure. Add that to the fact that stored passwords are a usability nightmare just waiting to happen. If the passwords are stored, the user probably will not remember them. If something happens to the SSO system, the user would probably end up needing to have all his passwords reset. Federated authentication goes a long way in mitigating these risks.

2.5.2.1.6 Ease Merger and Acquisition Activity

Federated identity can help in situations where two organizations need to integrate quickly. One of the most common cases of this is mergers and acquisitions. Traditionally, if you wanted to integrate two disparate organizations, you would have to migrate users from the credential store in one organization to the credential store in the other. This can take a lot of time. With federated identity, you can merge the two organizations without having to merge the two credential stores. If the two organizations have their own IdP, you can simply configure the applications at each organization to trust the IdP from the other organization. You can also configure a trust between the two IdPs and configure the appropriate translations if necessary.

2.5.2.1.7 Highly Extensible

Since the application itself does not know and generally does not care how the user was authenticated, you can use any method you choose for authentication. The IdP performs the authentication and then sends the appropriate information to the application. As long as the IdP sends the appropriate information to the application, it doesn't matter what method the IdP used to authenticate the user. The IdP can switch authentication methods used and it won't affect the authentication. If necessary you can also switch to a different IdP that uses the authentication method you desire. All you have to do is make sure the new IdP conforms to the standards and establish the appropriate trust.

2.5.2.2 Disadvantages

With all technologies, you have to take the good with the bad. Now that we have talked about the good, it's time to talk about the bad; this includes SSO issues, infrastructure requirements, and the newness of the technologies involved.

2.5.2.2.1 One Key to the Kingdom

One of the age-old objections to SSO is the "one key to the kingdom" theory. The idea is that if all your applications are protected by one set of credentials and that set of credentials is compromised, then the attacker would have access to all your applications. But if all your applications are credentialed separately, then the compromise of one password would only affect one application. In the case of federated identity, if the IdP is compromised or the user credentials that a user uses to log into the IdP are compromised, then an attacker would have access to all the user's applications. The risk is there, but given the cost to usability without a solution like federated identity, this risk is largely ignored nowadays.

2.5.2.2.2 Requires Specialized Infrastructure

Implementing a federated identity solution is not free. If you are establishing federated identity within your company, there are several things that must be done. First you have to establish an IdP. Then you have to configure your applications to use federated identity. The federated identity infrastructure setup will require hardware, software, and man-hours. With the recent restrictions in IT budgets, companies have to make sure they can justify the costs needed to implement the infrastructure. A lot of it will have to do with the number of applications that they will be able to connect to your infrastructure.

2.5.2.2.3 Need to Conform to Same Standards

Another limitation of federated identity solutions is that they need to conform to the same standards in order to interoperate. If you build a federated identity solution and it does not use the same protocols and standards as another solution, then most likely the two will not be able to interoperate. Ideally, you would be able to use the methods that worked best for your organization, but that's not always the case. You may have to give up a lot in terms of functionality and ease in order to gain the interoperability you need.

2.5.2.2.4 It's Really New

Federated identity isn't really a new concept, but it is somewhat unfamiliar, especially the new implementation methods and technologies used for federated identity. Federated identity suffers many of the challenges that are common to new technologies. Although the numbers are steadily increasing, there aren't many proven solutions or examples to go by. This makes it difficult to find guidance when you are trying to deploy your own solution.

Another issue is the lack of people with proven expertise in deploying federated identity solutions. Usually, if an organization lacks knowledge in a certain area, they can hire people or find contractors with the knowledge and experience in the area they need. This isn't really the case with federated identity. It's still hard to find potential employees or even contractors who have extensive knowledge or experience with this type of implementation.

There is also limited documentation available. Even for published solutions, the available documentation is often lacking the details an inexperienced professional would need. One of the most common ways of gathering information is through online research. A simple Internet search will return very few documented examples of federated identity implementations, so there is very little reference material that can be used for your implementation.

Finally, because of newness, there are a limited number of applications that currently support federated identity. Although adoption is slowly increasing, the lack of applications causes problems when expressing the value proposition of federated identity. Your organization may have a limited number of applications that use federated identity so the question that would arise is, how much value can be achieved by implementing a federated identity solution? If you choose to use a third-party IdP you incur a monthly fee. If you build an internal IdP you will incur implementation costs. Most of your applications might support another SSO method like Kerberos. Using Kerberos would generally be much cheaper than upgrading your applications to support federated identity functionality.

2.6 SUMMARY

Federated identity is based on a combination of several components including authentication, authorization, access control, IdPs, and service providers. Federated identity is not just about combining these components. It's also about how they are applied. With federated identity, authentication is abstracted from authorization. An IdP is used to authenticate users and provide identity information to service providers. The access control systems at the service provider then use this identity information to enforce authorization policies. If any of these components do not perform their job as described, you may have a robust infrastructure but you do not have federated identity.

CHAPTER 3

Federated Identity Technologies

Information in this chapter:

- OpenID
- OAuth
- Security Tokens
- Web Service Specifications
- Windows Identity Framework
- Claims-Based Identity

3.1 INTRODUCTION

In this chapter, we will be getting a little more technical. Now that you have a good general understanding of federated identity, we will cover the technologies that go into creating a federated identity solution. Most solutions use standard technologies for authentication, authorization, and security tokens. In this chapter, we will start by covering OpenID, OAuth, Simple Web Tokens (SWTs), JSON Web Token (JWT), and Security Assertion Markup Language (SAML). Next we will cover the specifications and extensions that bring federated identity security elements into everyday web applications. Then we will move into the technologies and frameworks that bring everything together. We will cover claims-based identity and the Windows Identity Framework.

3.2 OpenID

As we discussed in Chapter 2, identity providers (IdPs) authenticate users and then send their identity information to service providers. In order for this to work properly, the IdP and the service provider must speak the same language (Fig. 3.1). This is where OpenID comes in. OpenID provides a framework for information exchange between an IdP and a service provider. This allows the authentication process to be decoupled from the application or service without the fear of interoperability issues. As long as the service provider supports OpenID and the IdP adheres to the OpenID standard, the two providers should be able

Fig. 3.1. OpenID logo.

to work together. This leads us to one of the key features of OpenID. With OpenID, as long as the IdP adheres to the OpenID standard on the backend, it doesn't matter how the provider authenticates the user on the front-end. It could be username and password, one-time-use token, or any other method. It does not matter to the service provider as long as the IdP follows the specifications set by OpenID.

The OpenID standard is maintained by the OpenID Foundation. The OpenID Foundation is a nonprofit organization that consists of individual and corporate members from all over the world. This organization maintains all the copyrights and trademarks of OpenID. They are also responsible for supporting OpenID and responding to any issues that may arise, including security issues and deficiencies in the specification.

OpenID protocol messages are basically key-value pairs. All of keys in the message must be unique. However, there can be duplicate values. There are two modes the service provider can use to talk to the OpenID provider. They are checkid_setup and checkid_immediate. In checkid_setup, the end user communicates with the OpenID provider. In checkid_immediate, all communication between the service provider and the OpenID provider occurs without the end user's knowledge.

3.2.1 Using OpenID

The OpenID process starts with user registration. The user must choose an OpenID provider with whom to register. There are several OpenID providers available including Facebook, Google, and Yahoo. As part of the registration process, the user will enter their identity information. This may include first name, last name, age, address, and other personal information. Not all of this information, however, is transmitted from the IdP to the service provider. The user will have the option to specify which information they would like a particular service provider to be able to access.

What happens at the completion of the registration process depends on the version of OpenID supported by the IdP. With OpenID 1.0, a unique OpenID URL is generated for the user. This URL is used to identify the user. With OpenID 1.0, authentication to service provider can take place in one of two ways. The first is where the user enters their OpenID into the web site and the web redirects the user to the OpenID provider for authentication. Here is how it happens:

1. The user navigates to the destination web site that supports OpenID.
2. The user submits their OpenID to the web site.
3. The web site resolves the OpenID to obtain the address of the appropriate IdP.
4. The web redirects the user to the OpenID provider site.
5. The user authenticates to the OpenID provider site.
6. The IdP sends confirmation of the user's OpenID URL, along with any additional information selected by the user, back to the service provider.

The second scenario is where the target web site includes a link that allows the user to log in directly on the provider site. This is how that scenario happens:

1. The user navigates to the destination web site that supports OpenID.
2. On the login page, the user chooses the option for their service provider.
3. The web site redirects the user to the OpenID provider site.
4. The user authenticates to the OpenID provider site.
5. The IdP sends confirmation of the user's OpenID URL, along with any additional information selected by the user, back to the service provider.

With OpenID 2.0, an XRI may also be generated at the completion of registration. XRIs, or Extensible Resource Identifiers, come in two formats: i-names and i-numbers. The i-number is the permanent identifier that is used to identify the user. The i-name is mapped to the i-number but is not permanent. An i-name can be reassigned to different i-number if desired. The i-number is the identifier used by the service provider. If the service provider is sent an i-name, it will resolve it to the i-number, so that the i-number can be used.

In this scenario, authentication happens as follows:

1. The user navigates to the destination web site that supports OpenID.
2. The user submits their OpenID to the web site.
3. The web site requests an XRDS document to obtain the URL of the OpenID provider.
4. The web redirects the user to the OpenID provider site.
5. The user authenticates to the provider site.
6. The i-name or i-number is then sent back to the destination web site.

3.3 OAuth

Once you have authenticated, you need a means of providing authorization. This is where OAuth comes into play (Fig. 3.2). OAuth is an open standard for allowing secure authorization. With OAuth, a user can allow site A to access their information from site B. The key is that the user does not have to provide site A with his or her access credentials for site B. OAuth generates a token that site A can use to gain access to site B.

Several security considerations are taken when generating OAuth tokens. OAuth access tokens are not generalized tokens; they contain specific access information. The token will specify which site can be accessed, and what information can be accessed on that site. Any request that does not match these specifications will be denied. This prevents someone from intercepting an OAuth token from one site and using it on another site. In addition, OAuth tokens are only valid for a given interval. After the interval has passed, the user or application must obtain a new token. This helps to prevent replay attacks.

Fig. 3.2. OAuth logo.

3.3.1 Evolution of OAuth

Although OAuth has not been around very long, it has gone through a few revisions, most of which have been minor. We will cover four versions of OAuth: version 1.0, version 1.0a, OAuth WRAP, and version 2.0.

3.3.1.1 OAuth 1.0 and 1.0a

The OAuth discussion group was first started in 2007. It started because people were looking for a way to do access delegation. Some had originally thought that their OpenID implementations could be modified to handle delegation. But they realized that there were no standards for access delegation so if they wanted their implementations to be interoperable with others, then a new standard would have to be created. The OAuth Core 1.0 final draft was released in late 2007. This was the official start of the new standard that everyone was looking for. The OAuth 1.0 protocol was officially published in 2010.

OAuth defines three roles: client, server, and resource owner. You can think of the client as the client machine. The server is the service provider and the resource owner is the user. In the traditional client–server model, the client will access resources on the server. As long as the client can properly authenticate to the server, the client is allowed to access those resources.

OAuth uses a term called "legs" to describe its request methodology. The number of legs basically indicates how many parties are involved in a request. The two most common implementations are the three-legged model and the two-legged model. In the three-legged model, three distinct parties are involved: typically a resource owner, a client, and a server. In the two-legged model, the client is also the resource owner.

OAuth 1.0a came about in 2009. A security flaw was found in the "three-legged" model of OAuth. The flaw allowed for session fixation. Session fixation allows one user to set the session ID of another user. An attacker would not gain access to user credentials or OAuth tokens, but he would have access to the user session. OAuth 1.0a fixed this issue. The fix was eventually rolled back into the OAuth Core 1.0 specification before the final specification was published.

3.3.1.2 OAuth WRAP

WRAP is the Web Resource Authorization Protocol. WRAP is actually a profile designed for OAuth called OAuth WRAP. OAuth WRAP is used to allow users to grant applications access to their identity information. With the development of OAuth 2.0, OAuth WRAP has been deprecated but it is still in use.

OAuth WRAP uses token exchange to secure access. To further secure communications, OAuth WRAP communications are done using SSL. In OAuth WRAP, the client will obtain a bearer token from the Authorization Server. This token will have a specified lifetime that is usually very short. The client will then present this token to the server hosting the desired resource. WRAP also allows for a client to act on another user's behalf. OAuth WRAP also provides for refresh tokens that are used to obtain new tokens before expiration.

The OAuth WRAP authentication process is as follows:

1. The user attempts to access an application.
2. The user is redirected to the IdP to receive a verification code.
3. The user gives consent for the application to access information from the IdP.
4. The user submits the verification code to the application.
5. The application uses the verification code to contact the IdP.
6. The IdP returns an access token and a refresh token to the application.
7. The application uses the access token to retrieve user data.
8. When the access token expires, the application uses the refresh token to get a new access token.

3.3.1.3 OAuth 2.0

OAuth 2.0 is the newest version of OAuth, currently in development. OAuth 2.0 is being done through the Internet Engineering Task Force (IETF)'s OAuth Working Group. It's attempting to improve some of the shortcomings of OAuth 1.0. Its two main goals are security and interoperability. Currently, it's not compatible with previous versions of OAuth.

OAuth 2.0 introduces six new flows: user-agent flow, web server flow, device flow, username and password flow, client credentials flow, and assertion flow. OAuth 2.0 also introduces the concept of bearer tokens. Instead of using cryptography, these tokens are used as the secret to secure the communications between systems.

3.4 SECURITY TOKENS

Security tokens are a key component in federated identity deployments. Security tokens are the vehicles used to pass information back and forth between IdPs and service providers. The architecture of the security token will determine what information can be passed and how the information will be passed. Some security token architectures focus on simplicity; some focus on robustness. We will cover three of the more commonly used architectures: Simple Web Tokens (SWTs), JSON Web Tokens (JWTs), and Security Assertion Markup Language (SAML) tokens. As we will see, each token has its own usage and benefits.

3.4.1 Simple Web Tokens

SWTs use a very simple format for transmitting assertions. SWT assertions consist of name/value pairs. Because of this simple format, SWTs are very lightweight. They are often used in HTTP headers and other places where space is limited.

3.4.1.1 SWT Attributes

In SWTs, the name/value pairs are called attributes. SWTs have one mandatory name/value pair: HMACSHA256, which is always the last name/value pair in the token. The value is the SHA256 HMAC of the other name/value pairs in the token.

> **Note**
>
> A MAC is a message authentication code. Method authentication codes are used to verify the authenticity and the integrity of a message. An HMAC uses a hash function in conjunction with a cryptographic key to create the MAC. HMACs can use a variety of hash functions. An HMACSHA256 uses a SHA256 hash.

SWTs have three reserved attribute names. These attributes are reserved, but they are not mandatory. They are as follows:

- *Issuer*—identifies the issuer of the token.
- *ExpiresOn*—specifies a date after which the token should no longer be accepted.
- *Audience*—identifies the audience that the token is intended for.

SWTs make use of public name attributes. Public name attributes are registered names that are publicly declared so that systems know not to use them. Public names can be defined using a reverse DNS name or a URI (Uniform Resource Identifier)

SWTs also make use of private name attributes. Private name attributes are attributes that are defined by the system in which they are implemented. An SWT issuer and consumer can agree on a set of private names to use. You can use any names you want, except for reserved names. You have to take caution when using private names, because they are subject to collisions since they can be used by anyone for any purpose.

3.4.2 JSON Web Tokens

A JWT is a method for representing claims. JWTs use a compact format that is often used in HTTP Authorization headers and URI queries. In a JWT, the claims are encoded as a JSON object. The tokens are then encoded using Base64 encoding. JWTs are digitally signed using a JSON web signature (JWS). For additional security, JWTs can also be encrypted using JSON Web Encryption, or JWE.

3.4.2.1 JWT Components

JWTs have three parts that are separated by a period. They are the JWT header, the JWT second part, and the JWT third part. These part names may sound generic, but there is a reason for that. Depending on how the token is constructed and whether it is signed or encrypted, the contents of the parts may change.

The JWT header describes the cryptographic operations used within the token. When the token is signed, the JWT header is a JWS header. When the token is encrypted, the JWT header is a JWE header. When the JWT is signed, the JWT second part is the encoded JWS payload. When the JWT is encrypted, the JWT second part is the encoded JWE encrypted key. When the JWT is signed, the JWT third part is the encoded JWS signature. When the JWT is encrypted, the JWT third part is the encoded JWT ciphertext.

3.4.2.2 JWT Claims

The JWT Claims Set is a string that contains the claims set in the token. The JWT Claims Set consists of claim pairs that include the Claim

Name and a corresponding Claim Value. The Claim Names within a JWT must all be unique. But, different Claim Names can have the same Claim Value. JWTs consist of three different types of claims: Reserved Claim Names, Public Claim Names, and Private Claim Names.

Several reserved claim names have been specified in the definition of JWT. They are a set of claims intended to make the use of JWT easier. The following are Reserved Claim Names:

- exp—specifies an expiration time for the token.
- nbf—specifies a time before which the token is not valid.
- iat—specifies when the token was issued.
- iss—identifies the issuer of the token.
- aud—identifies the audience for whom the token is intended.
- prn—identifies the principle, or the subject of the token.
- jti—used to specify a unique identifier for the token.
- typ—used to specify a type for the contents of the Claim Set.

In order to prevent a collision between Claim Names used by different implementations, there is the concept of Pubic Claim Names. You can register a claim with the Internet Assigned Numbers Authority (IANA) JWT Claims registry, or you can define the claim as a URI.

Private Claim Names are names you use that are not registered. You have to be careful when using Private Claim Names because they are more susceptible to collisions.

3.4.2.3 JWT Creation

There are two ways to determine if the JWT is signed or encrypted. The first is by looking at the algorithm (alg) value in the header. If the value is a signature algorithm then the JWT is a JWS. If the value is an encryption algorithm, then the JWT is a JWE. The second way is to check for an enc member. If one is present then the JWT is a JWE. If not, then the JWT is a JWS.

JWTs can also be created in plain text. This is for cases where they are secured by some other external method. When the JWT is plaintext, the alg value must be set to none. Plaintext JWTs are formatted the same as a signed JWT. The only difference is that it contains an empty signature.

3.4.3 Security Assertion Markup Language

SAML is an XML-based standard for sending authentication and identity information. One of the reasons it has taken so long for a common Internet authentication standard to be developed is because it was hard to get agreement on the method or format used for sharing the user information. There were many attempts made at finding this common format. Some of the methods were new and some were adaptations on existing protocols, but none of them stuck. Only a few companies and vendors agreed to adopt this protocol but not enough to obtain a critical mass.

Then along came SAML. SAML's main purpose was to solve this information exchange problem. In the beginning stages of SAML, it faced many of the same challenges that methods before it had faced. It was hard to get buy-in. In many cases, it meant that some vendors would have to change their architectures; and they were reluctant to do so. Some pointed to deficiencies in the SAML protocol. Some just refused to give up on the work they had already invested. But as the SAML standard has matured, it gained more and more traction. Now, SAML v2 has become the standard that we were waiting for.

3.4.3.1 SAML Components

SAML is more than just a standard. It's a collection of standards. SAML has four main components: SAML assertions, SAML protocols, SAML bindings, and SAML profiles.

3.4.3.1.1 SAML Assertions

SAML uses assertions to make user identity statements. These statements are what are used by the service provider to make decisions. There are three types of SAML assertions: authentication statements, attribute statements, and authorization decision statements.

Authentication statement assertions let the service provider know the user or principle authenticated with the IdP and the time the authentication occurred. They may also include information about what method was used to authenticate. An assertion may also include the authentication context. The authentication context is just additional information describing the circumstances about how the user authenticated. Attribute statement assertions carry information about the user, e.g., the user's first and last name. Attribute statement assertions come in the form of a name value pair. Authorization decision statement assertions govern what actions a given principle is allowed to perform. For example, user1 can read file xyz.

3.4.3.1.2 SAML Protocols

SAML protocols are request/response protocols. The protocols define how elements must be formulated in SAML requests and responses. SAML protocols also give rules for producing and consuming these elements.

SAML protocol requests are called queries. Service providers make queries directly to IdPs. The responses are generally sent back in the form of assertions. There are three main types of queries: authentication query, attribute query, and authorization decision query.

3.4.3.1.3 SAML Bindings

SAML bindings are when SAML messages are mapped to common communication protocols. For example, SAML is often used with the SOAP protocol.

3.4.3.1.4 SAML Profiles

SAML profiles are a combination of SAML assertions, protocols, and bindings. SAML profiles are usually defined for a particular purpose or use case.

3.4.3.2 The Evolution of SAML

In order to have a good understanding of SAML, it's important to understand how the standard got to where it is today. Each version of SAML added different assertions, protocols, bindings, and profiles. The previous versions of SAML, although important in understanding the evolution, aren't as important in understanding how SAML is currently implemented. So we will just cover the previous versions briefly. We will spend most of our time with the current version, SAML v2.0.

3.4.3.2.1 SAML v1.0

SAML was first developed by an OASIS committee. OASIS, or the Organization for the Advancement of Structured Information Standards, is a consortium that helps drive web standards. OASIS wanted to come up with a standard for exchanging authentication and authorization information over the web. In 2002, SAML became an OASIS standard. This original standard outlined the components we just discussed.

3.4.3.2.2 SAML v1.1

The next version of SAML was SAML v1.1. SAML 1.1 was ratified by OASIS in 2003. SAML 1.1 did not make any changes to assertions nor did it specify any additional protocols. SAML 1.1 only defines one binding: the SAML SOAP binding. This is a synchronous protocol. SAML is implemented over SOAP, which is implemented over HTTP. With the SAML SOAP binding, SAML requests and responses are wrapped inside the body of SOAP messages. The SAML 1.1 specification outlined two profiles: the Browser/Artifact profile and the Browser/POST profile.

- *Browser/Artifact Profile*—The Browser/Artifact profile uses a pull mechanism. SSO assertions are passed from the IdP to the service provider as a reference. This reference is done through the browser using an HTTP redirect. The service provider then pulls the SSO information from the IdP.
- *Browser/POST Profile*—The Browser/POST profile uses a push mechanism to send SSO information as values.

3.4.3.2.3 SAML 2.0

SAML v2.0 was established as an OASIS standard is 2005. It is very different from its predecessors. SAML v2.0 adds a host of new protocols and bindings specification.

3.4.3.2.3.1 SAML 2.0 Assertions

SAML 2.0 includes a "bearer" assertion. This assertion is used for SSO within a web browser session. It contains both an authentication statement and an attribute statement.

SAML v2.0 supports the following protocols:

- *Assertion Query and Request Protocol*—This query is used to request SAML assertions that have already been made. The query can be based on a reference, subject, or statement type.
- *Authentication Request Protocol*—In SAML 2.0, flows are initiated by the service provider sending an authentication request to the IdP. The <saml:AuthnRequest> element is sent to the IdP.
- *Artifact Resolution Protocol*—An artifact is a reference to a SAML message. This protocol allows you to retrieve a previously created assertion by using a reference. SAML can refer to an assertion by an artifact. Then the service provider can use the artifact and the Artifact Resolution protocol to retrieve the assertion.

- *Name Identifier Management Protocol*—This protocol can be used to change the name or the name format of a principle. It can also be used to terminate a name association between an IdP and a service provider. The IdP or the service provider can use this protocol to issue requests.
- *Single Logout Protocol*—This protocol allows you to create a request to logout all the sessions associated with a given principle at once. The logout can be initiated by the principle or by a timeout.
- *Name Identifier Mapping Protocol*—This protocol provides a mechanism to allow accounts to be linked for federation.

The following bindings are supported with SAML 2.0:

- *SAML SOAP Binding*—This binding is the same as it was in SAML 1.1.
- *Reverse SOAP Binding (also called PAOS Binding)*—With this binding, an HTTP requester can advertise the ability to act as a SOAP responder or SOAP intermediary.
- *HTTP Redirect Binding*—This binding defines a method where SAML messages can be transmitted using URL parameters. It may be used with the HTTP POST or HTTP Artifact bindings.
- *HTTP POST Binding*—This binding defines a method where SAML messages may be transmitted within an HTML form control. It may be used with the HTTP Redirect and HTTP Artifact bindings.
- *HTTP Artifact Binding*—With this binding, the SAML request and the SAML response are transmitted using a reference. The reference is called an artifact. A separate binding is used to exchange the artifact.
- *SAML URI Binding*—This binding supports the encapsulation of a <samlp:AssertionIDRequest> message with a single <samlAssertionIDRef> into a URI. This binding is transport independent.

SAML v2.0 also adds a host of new profiles. They are as follows:

- *Web Browser SSO Profile*—The Browser Artifact and Browser POST profiles were combined to create one Web Browser SSO profile. This profile uses the SAML Authentication Request protocol with the HTTP Redirect, HTTP POST, and HTTP Artifact bindings.

- *Enhanced Client or Proxy Profile*—This is a system entity that is used to determine which IdP to contact. The profile is based on the SAML Authentication Request protocol and the PAOS binding.
- *Identity Provider Discovery Profile*—The Identity Provider Discovery Profile introduces four concepts: the common domain, the common domain cookie, the common domain cookie reading service, and the common domain cookie writing service. The common domain is an upper level domain to which multiple subdomains belong. The common domain cookie is a secure browser cookie whose scope is the common domain. The common domain cookie maintains a history of the IdPs a user has recently visited. When a service provider receives an unauthenticated request, it will send a request to the common domain cookie reading service to read the most recently visited IdP. After the user successfully authenticates to an IdP, the IdP will make a request to the common domain cookie writing service to append the IdP's unique identity to the common domain cookie.
- *Single Logout Profile*—Name Identifier Management Profile.
- *Artifact Resolution Profile*—This profile resolves SAML artifacts into a protocol message.
- *Assertion Query/Request Profile*—This profile is a somewhat generic profile that is used to make queries using certain SAML elements. These elements are:
  - AssertionIDRequest—used to request an assertion by supplying its unique identifier.
  - SubjectQuery—allows the use of subject-based SAML queries.
  - AuthnQuery—used to request existing authentication assertions about a subject.
  - AttributeQuery—used to request attributes about a subject.
  - AuthzDecisionQuery—used to request an authorization decision.
- *Name Identifier Mapping Profile*—This profile defines the use of the Name Identifier Mapping protocol with a synchronous binding.
- *SAML Attribute Profiles*—This basic profile is used for naming SAML attributes and values. It eliminates the need for extension schemas.

3.5 WEB SERVICE SPECIFICATIONS

Web Service Specifications, also called WS-* specifications, lay out a framework for designing, building, and protecting web services.

Although these specifications were developed by members from different vendors, the specifications themselves are designed to be vendor-agnostic. There are many different specifications that help guide you in your work with web services. We will focus on the security-related specifications that are applicable to a federated identity environment. We will cover WS-Security, WS-SecurityPolicy, WS-SecureConversation, WS-Trust, and WS-Federation.

3.5.1 WS-Security

WS-Security was designed to enhance the security of web service communications. The WS-Security specification has three components: SOAP message security, the Username Token Profile, and the x.509 certificate token profile. The SOAP message security component is an extension to the SOAP protocol used to secure communications with web services. It allows for authentication, integrity, and confidentiality. The UserName Token Profile allows a web service consumer to supply a username token to a web service as a means of identification. The x.509 certificate token profile allows a digital certificate to be used to validate a public key that can in turn be used to authenticate a SOAP message.

3.5.2 WS-SecurityPolicy

WS-SecurityPolicy specifies security policies than can be applied to WS-Security, WS-SecureConversation, and WS-Trust. WS-Security describes a set of assertions that can be made to secure the messages. The policies will dictate which parts of a message will be secured, any preconditions, the security mechanism, token types, and trust options.

3.5.3 WS-SecureConversation

WS-SecureConversion is an extension to WS-Secure. It defines methods for establishing security contexts. These security contexts are then used to derive session keys. The session keys are used to secure the communication session.

3.5.4 WS-Trust

WS-Trust is an extension to the WS-Security specification. WS-Trust deals with issuing, renewing, and validating security tokens. WS-Trust establishes the trust relationship between the agents in message exchanges. This means that the two parties in exchange must trust each other. WS-Trust defines a token exchange that is used to establish this trust. WS-Trust defines the message formats in token requests and responses, and the mechanisms for key exchange.

3.5.5 WS-Federation

WS-Federation is an extension to the WS-Security specification. WS-Federation can be used by web services and SOAP clients. WS-Federation allows two security realms to set up a federated trust. This trust allows users in one realm to access resources in the other realm. WS-Federated allows for the brokering of assertions related to authentication, authorization, and identity.

3.6 WINDOWS IDENTITY FOUNDATION

Windows Identity Foundation, or WIF, is a framework created by Microsoft for developing claims-based applications and token services. WIF is part of Microsoft's Federated Identity software family. WIF is a collection of .NET Framework classes. Instead of developers having to directly code against frameworks like WS-Trust and WS-Federation, they can just code against the WIF framework. WIF is built around WS-Trust and WS-Federation and exposes APIs that developers can code against.

WIF has templates built into newer versions of Visual Studio. These templates are for creating ASP.NET web sites and Windows Communication Foundation (WCF) Services. This makes it much easier to develop claims-based applications and services.

There are a couple of very useful utilities that are included with WIF. The first is FedUtil. FedUtil is used to quickly establish trusts between a relying party and an STS. FedUtil is also included in Visual Studio, so it can be accessed from the solution explorer. The other utility is a service called Claims to Windows Token Service, or c2WTS. C2WTS does token translations between claims tokens and NT tokens. This allows users of claims-based applications to be able to access NT token-based backend applications.

Microsoft uses WIF as the basis for claims-based applications and products it develops; the most notable of which are Active Directory Federation Services (ADFS) 2.0 and Access Control Services (ACS). ADFS 2.0 provides a claims-based identity infrastructure. ADFS 2.0 is a downloadable component that is installed on Windows-based servers. ACS is a Windows Azure-based service for authentication and access control.

3.6.1 WIF Features

The WIF framework provides a complete set of features based on WS-Trust and WS-Federation. You can use WIF to implement the functionality provided by these two protocols, without needing to have knowledge of how to implement them directly. The most commonly used features and usage scenarios for WIF are in the areas of application development, identity delegation, the ability to create custom token servers, and step-up authentication.

3.6.1.1 Claims-Aware Applications

The most common use of WIF is building claims-aware applications. It provides a claims model and a framework for making access decisions based on claims. WIF also provides a consistent programming environment whether you're developing using ASP.NET or WCF.

3.6.1.2 Identity Delegation

WIF provides support for building identity delegation into claims-aware applications. WIF can maintain the requester's identity across different service boundaries. This means that when a service or application makes a request on behalf of the original requestor, the requester's identity is passed along with the request. For example, let's say application ABC needs to access a backend database. After user1 logs into application ABC, the backend database access requests are made using the identity of user1. This allows you to configure specific user permissions on the database. In many other instances, a service account is used to access the backend database. In scenarios like this, the service account would need full access to the database. User-based permissions could only be managed through the application. This is considered to be a less secure deployment model.

3.6.1.3 Custom Token Servers

WIF provides the ability to build a custom Secure Token Server, or STS. You can build an active STS or a passive STS. An active STS is based on the WS-Trust protocol and is generally used by web services. A passive STS is based on the WS-Federation protocol and is generally used for web-browser-based applications.

3.6.1.4 Step-Up Authentication

In step-up authentication, a single application may require multiple layers of authentication. You may use one type of authentication for initial login, then another type of authentication for accessing a specific feature or function within an application.

3.7 CLAIMS-BASED IDENTITY

In this section, we will be covering claims-based identity, also called claims-based authentication, or CBA. Claims-based authentication is one of the more popular implementation methods of federated identity. In fact CBA is used as the basis for Microsoft's ADFS 2.0 implementation.

3.7.1 CBA Description and Overview

Claims-based identity, like federation, has been around a long time. Also, like federation, it is just now gaining widespread usage. This usage has been driven by the uptake in web-based applications and web-based services. The three main components of the claims-based identity architecture are the issuer, the token, and the claim. We will get into each of these components individually in a minute, but first I'll tell you how they work together. It starts with the claim. A set of claims will be wrapped into a single token. This token will be created and distributed by the issuer:

1. The user authenticates to the issuer.
2. The issuer issues a token to the user.
3. The user presents his token to the application.
4. The application examines the claims within the token and makes decisions accordingly.

3.7.1.1 Claims

As you can probably guess, the claim is the centerpiece of claim-based identity. So, what exactly is a claim? To put it simply, a claim is a statement made about a subject. The statement could be a name, group membership, or anything that identifies the subject. These claims are what the receiving system uses to make decisions.

Claims are a very powerful mechanism for transmitting user attributes. In a traditional authentication system, usually the only attributes that are transmitted during the authentication process are username and password. This is because traditional authentication tokens only support these attributes. If other attributes are needed by the application, these attributes must be obtained by another separate request. Usually, this means the application itself would need access to the attributes. This means the application would not only need to be aware of where the attributes are, but also how to access them.

In a CBA implementation, claims are taken from the attribute store. The attribute store can be a database, Active Directory, or some other directory store. The attribute can be the same as the credential store, or it can be an entirely different store. The attribute store will contain a mapping of users to different attributes. When the authentication process takes place, the appropriate attributes are read from the store and turned into claims. These claims are sent as part of the authentication process. There is no need for an application to make a direct call to the attribute store.

3.7.1.2 Token
In order for claims to be sent from one system to another, they need some type of transport and delivery mechanism. This is where tokens come in. Claims are passed around in the form of a token. A token can contain a single claim or multiple claims. A token will also contain a digital signature. The signature is used to identify the issuer that issued the token. This is so an application can know which token authority created the token.

Tokens can be created using a few different formats. SAML is quickly becoming the standard for authentication tokens, but there are other options. The SWT format is also a commonly used format. The JWT format is also another option. You have to make sure that the applications you are interacting with understand the format you are using for the tokens.

3.7.1.3 Issuer
The issuer is the entity that creates and digitally signs all the tokens. The issuer is responsible for pulling the information from the attribute store and putting them into the token as claims. Each issuer must choose a format to use for creating tokens.

In most cases, the issuer will also serve as an IdP. In addition to creating tokens, it will also perform the authentication so the issuer does not only need to talk to the attribute store, but also to the credential store.

3.7.1.3.1 Secure Token Server

In a claims-based identity system, the central issuing authority is called the STS. In most cases, the STS will also act as an IdP. It must be configured to point to the authentication store. It also must be configured to point to an attribute store.

As the issuer, the STS cannot be used by just any application. The STS needs to be configured with a URI for each application that will redirect to it.

3.7.1.3.1.1 CBA Authentication Process

1. User attempts to access an application.
2. User is redirected to the STS.
3. User authenticates to the STS.
4. The STS pulls claim information from the appropriate store and uses the information to create a token.
5. The token is sent back to the user.
6. Token is submitted to application.

3.7.1.4 The Application

We can't forget the application. After all, the application is what the user is trying to gain access to. Although it is not a part of the CBA infrastructure, the application is a part of the CBA process. The application is also called the relying party. This is because the application relies on the STS and the claims created by it. The application itself will not process any authentication requests or accept any authentication information. This is reserved for the STS. If the STS is not functioning properly, then the application cannot be accessed.

Applications don't just automatically accept claims-based identity information. They must be configured to do so. CBA does not work with all applications. Instead, applications must be configured with the capability to properly process information from an STS. The application must also be configured with the information of any STS that it will accept tokens from. The STS needs to include the appropriate claims needed by the application in the token.

In order for the application to properly interact with the STS, there are certain components that must be in place and rules that must be followed. One component that must be a part of an application in order for it to support claims-based identity is the identity library. The identity library is a set of code that performs several functions. One of the jobs of the identity library is to verify the token's signature. It will pull out the name of the issuer, then it will ensure that the issuer that signed the token is a trusted issuer. The application is configured with a trusted issuer. If the issuer that sent the token is not a trusted issuer, then the token will not be accepted. The rules that need to be followed are generally dictated by the type of token used by the application. For example, if the application is configured to accept SAML tokens, then the STS must be configured dispense SAML tokens. SAML itself defines certain rules that must be adhered to when the application and the STS are interacting with each other.

3.7.2 Active and Passive Clients

Claims-based authentication implementations require a client application for requesting tokens and submitting tokens to applications. In a claims-based authentication environment, there are two types of clients: active clients and passive clients. They each serve a different purpose and work in different scenarios. Not all organizations that use claims-based authentication will use both types of clients. You have to figure out what the needs of your organization are, and then make a decision as to the type of clients you want to deploy.

3.7.2.1 Passive Clients

Passive clients are the most common type of CBA client. Passive client scenarios are mainly used for web applications. Passive clients use the web browser as the client application for requesting and submitting tokens. Passive clients are generally considered the easiest type of CBA clients to implement because they don't require any additional coding or configuration on the client side. Everything needed to work in a CBA environment is already built into the browser. The only downside is that passive CBA clients require user interaction, thus limiting the number of scenarios where they can provide functionality (Fig. 3.3).

3.7.2.1.1 Passive Client Flow
1. User attempts to access resource.
2. Resource redirects browser to STS URL.
3. Browser redirects to STS URL.

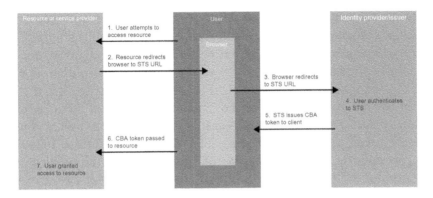

Fig. 3.3. Passive CBA flow.

4. User authenticates to STS.
5. STS issues token to client.
6. Token is passed to resource.
7. User is granted access to resource.

3.7.2.2 Active Clients

Active CBA clients can provide expanded functionality over passive clients because they do not require user interaction. Active clients are usually used for entities like web services. One of the big advantages of active clients is the ability to use user credentials to access backend resources like databases. For example, a user would first log into an application, then the active CBA client can get a CBA token for the user, which is used to access the backend database.

Active clients are a little more complicated to implement than passive clients. In order to make use of an active client scenario, you must develop your own client to request and manage the CBA tokens. The WIF framework will provide you with the tools you will need for the development of an active client (Fig. 3.4).

3.7.2.2.1 Active Client Flow
1. Username used to request CBA token.
2. STS authenticates user.
3. CBA token issues to application.
4. Call made to web service using token.
5. WIF validates security token.
6. Response returned.

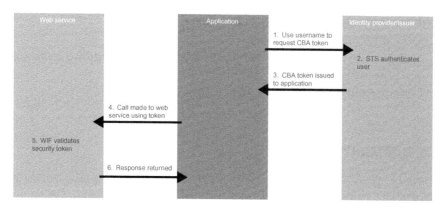

Fig. 3.4. Active CBA flow.

3.7.3 Cross-Realm Federation with CBA

As we've seen, each application must be configured with an issuer. This issuer is the one that creates the tokens that will be trusted by the application. So what happens when an application trusts one issuer but a user logs into a different issuer? How can the user still use the application? The answer is cross-realm federation.

Cross-realm federation allows you to log into one STS and access applications that are configured for another STS. There are many situations where this might be the case. You might have a situation where you have an application that is accessed by customers or partners, but you don't want to manage user accounts for those users. You can have the users log into a separate IdP but still allow them access to your application. You may also have a situation where your organization has acquired a new company. This company already had their own IdP. If you need to provide these users access to your company's applications, you don't have to wait until you port all the users over to your IdP. They can still log into their own IdP and have access to your company's applications.

You can set up a federation trust between two issuers. In addition to configuring the trust, you have to configure a token translation. With a token translation, you configure the incoming claim and what the outbound claim should be changed to.

1. User attempts to access application.
2. User is redirected to issuer1 configured on application.
3. User selects issuer2 for authentication.

4. User authenticates to issuer2 and receives token.
5. User presents token to issuer1.
6. Issuer1 converts token to one that can be used by applications and send that token to user.
7. User presents new token to application.

3.8 SUMMARY

OpenID provides a specification for standardized authentication. OAuth provides a framework for authorization. SWTs and JWTs are much simpler than SAML tokens. They do not offer as much functionality but are much smaller. Because of this, they are often used when space is limited, such as HTTP headers. SAML provides a very robust framework for creating and transmitting tokens. SAML tokens can be a little heavy and somewhat difficult to implement, compared to other options, but they provide the best security and are the most flexible. The WIF provides an easy way to code against the Web Service Specifications needed for claims-based identity. The WIF framework was used to develop ADFS 2.0 and Windows Azure ACS. Claims-based authentication is one of the most widely used federated identity implementation technologies; it is used as the basis for many solutions, including Microsoft ADFS 2.0

CHAPTER 4

Deployment Options

Information in this chapter:

- Making a Choice
- ADFS
- ACS

4.1 INTRODUCTION

There are a lot of options available when looking at federated identity solutions and deployments. The first choice you must make is whether to go with an internal solution or an external hosted solution. The next choice you must make is to decide which implementation or product to go with. In this chapter, we will start by going over the criteria you should look at when making your choice. Then we will cover two of the most commonly used options: Active Directory Federation Services (ADFS) and Microsoft Azure Access Control Services (ACS).

4.2 MAKING A CHOICE

Choosing the right federated identity solution or solutions can be difficult. One of the big choices you have to make when considering a federated identity solution is whether to go with an on-premise solution or an off-premise solution. You can choose a hosted issuer that you control or an issuer that you don't control. Each option has its own advantages and disadvantages. In some cases, organizations end up with a combination of both.

You will have to try to do some future planning. You should make sure that the solution you choose will be your needs today and in the future, as your use of federated identity is likely to grow. Some of the options you will want to look at are flexibility, maintenance, availability, security, and cost.

4.2.1 Flexibility

From a configuration standpoint, an on-premise solution is likely to be more flexible as it enables better control over the configuration. This allows you to take full advantage of the features offered by the solution. Providers have a lot more environments that need to be maintained so they will often simplify the feature set of their offering to make administration and maintenance easier. If the implementation you need is fairly simple, then the options provided by a solution provider may fit your needs.

On some occasions, you may find that a service provider may be able to offer more options when it comes to things like the attribute store or the authentication provider. Many service providers will already have built-in support for an array of different stores. Depending on the solution you select at your organization, you may be able to build in the same type of support, but it might require more time/work than you are willing to invest.

4.2.2 Management and Maintenance

Maintenance can definitely be an issue with internal solutions, especially customized solutions. With hosted solutions, the service provider will be responsible for maintenance, but if you deploy an internal solution, you will be responsible for maintenance. If you choose to go with a completely custom solution, you will be responsible for obtaining all patches and doing all upgrades yourself. If you have highly specialized needs, you may choose a customized out-of-the-box solution. With this option, you will be able to get most updates and patches from the vendor, but you run the risk that your customizations may not be automatically carried forward when you upgrade. If this is the case, you may have to redo some or all of the customization in the new, upgraded platform.

Federated identity providers (IdPs) will generally consist of an authentication store and an attribute store. Whoever is responsible for the IdP is responsible for managing these two stores. One of the biggest management burdens comes from managing the authentication store. Along with general system maintenance, the management of the authentication store also requires user management. User management includes tasks like account and password resets. These seemingly small tasks can really add up in a large environment. If you select an external IdP, you don't have to worry about your service desk having to perform these maintenance tasks. Instead, they would be the responsibility of the service provider, which would assist in controlling help desk costs. Depending on the terms of your contract, the provider may charge you for performing these and other user management tasks.

4.2.3 Availability

When it comes to federated identity, or any identity or authentication solution, availability is extremely important. If the authentication system is not available, then users will not be able to access the applications or services they need. If you go with a hosted solution, you should ensure that the infrastructure is located in different datacenters in different locations. Many people take for granted that if they go with a hosted solution, they will be protected. The truth is that many service providers have all of their infrastructure and systems in one location. If there is a problem at the location, then you will not be able to access their services. Even with service providers who have a presence in multiple locations, you still have to do your due diligence investigations. Sometimes, even though the provider has a presence in multiple locations, the systems that provide your service will not be housed in multiple locations unless you specifically ask for that and it is specifically written in your contract.

If you go with an internal solution, depending on how your organization is structured, you may or may not have the option of placing your infrastructure in multiple locations. Internally you may or may not have the option of locating the infrastructure in multiple locations. If you do, it would be highly recommended, and well worth any increase in your overall costs.

4.2.4 Security

Security should always be a primary concern when dealing with identity. You want to make sure that credentials and identity information are properly stored and transmitted. In most cases, you should actually look to minimize the number of times credentials are passed between systems. This is one of the primary benefits of federated identity. However, there are times when you can't avoid sending credentials even in a federated identity implementation. That number should be kept to a minimum.

You need to ensure the system itself is safe. In a federated identity solution, information will be passed back and forth between different systems and different services on these systems. When examining your solution, you need to make sure the system and services involved require some type of authentication before sensitive information is passed.

4.2.5 Cost

Obviously, cost is a factor in all implementation. There are two types of costs you must deal with: capital and expense. Most solutions will be higher in one area than the other. For the most part, internal solutions will cost more in capital because of the hardware and software costs associated with implementing a new solution. In general, going with an external solution provider will have higher ongoing expense costs. Depending on your organization's budgeting concerns, the solution that makes sense from a functional and technical perspective may not make sense from a financial perspective. You need to understand your organization's cost constraints before you make your final decision.

4.3 ACTIVE DIRECTORY FEDERATION SERVICES

Active Directory Federation Services (ADFS) is an enterprise-level identity and access management system. ADFS 2.0 is Microsoft's implementation of claims-based identity infrastructure. ADFS 2.0 was built using the Windows Identity Foundation framework. This framework allows ADFS 2.0 to grow as the framework grows. It also allows ADFS 2.0 to make use of the features and functionality integrated into the framework. ADFS 2.0 is installed as an add-on component to your Windows 2008-based or higher servers that can be downloaded from the Microsoft web site.

> There is an ADFS role available on Windows 2008 servers, but it installs an older version of ADFS. If you want to use ADFS 2.0, you have to use the download file for installation.

4.3.1 ADFS 2.0 Functionality

ADFS 2.0 adds a lot of functionality over what was previously supported with ADFS. ADFS 2.0 uses a true claim-based approach to authentication, authorization, and federation. ADFS takes a standards-based approach to implementing functionality. This allows greater interoperability with other token services and claims-based IdPs.

4.3.1.1 Claims-Based Authentication Clients

ADFS 2.0 provides full claims-based authentication (CBA) functionality by supporting both active and passive clients. Passives clients generally use in web-site-based activities. Most web browsers have built-in passive CBA client functionality. Active clients are a little bit different; they are mostly used with web services. Active CBA clients are usually developed using the Windows Identity Foundation framework.

4.3.1.2 SAML

In order to provide standard token support, ADFS 2.0 supports the use of Security Assertion Markup Language (SAML) 2.0. This allows it to be compatible with a wide range of federation technologies. It can interoperate with virtually any implementation that adheres to the SAML 2.0 standard.

4.3.1.3 Federation with Other STSs

ADFS 2.0 supports federation with other Secure Token Servers (STSs). This allows you to trust tokens that were generated by another issuer. The federation server will then perform a token transformation. The federation server will pull the claims from the incoming token and use them to create tokens of its own. The new token can then be used by relying parties that trust your STS.

4.3.2 ADFS 2.0 Components

An ADFS 2.0 implementation includes several key components. Each component plays a different role in providing the total solution. We will cover each of these components. They include the federation servers, the attribute store, relying parties, and endpoints.

4.3.2.1 Federation Service

The Federation Service is one of the key components of an ADFS 2.0 environment. The Federation Service serves several purposes. The federation server is the server that manages the tokens. Basically, it's the server where the STS is installed. The Federation Service manages the trust relationship with the relying parties. It also manages the trust relationship with other IdPs. The federation server can be configured using the Federation Server Configuration Wizard or the fsconfig tool.

4.3.2.2 Federation Proxy Servers

Federation Proxy Servers allow external users access to your internal ADFS 2.0 environment. A Federation Proxy Server can be installed in your DMZ. External users will authenticate against the proxy. The proxy will forward the requests to your internal Federation Server. This allows you to authenticate external users without having to let unauthenticated traffic into your internal network.

4.3.2.3 Attribute Stores

The attribute store is where the values used for the claims are stored. After authentication, the STS will query the attribute store to find the appropriate user information needed to set the claims and create the token. Although ADFS 2.0 only supports using Active Directory as the authentication store, you can use Active Directory, LDAP, SQL, or a custom store for the attribute store.

4.3.2.4 Relying Parties

The relying party is the consumer of the claims created by the STS. Since ADFS 2.0 supports both active and passive clients, the relying parties can be web applications or web services. The STS must be configured with the configuration information for each relying party that it will support.

4.3.2.5 Endpoints

Endpoints are used to provide access to services on the federation server. There are several types of endpoints that can be used with ADFS 2.0 including WS-Trust 1.3, WS-Trust 2005, WS-Federation Passive, SAML SS0, Federation Metadata, SAML Artifact Resolution, and WS-Trust WSDL.

4.3.3 ADFS 2.0 Federation Server Configuration Wizard

Before you can begin using ADFS 2.0, you must first configure your federation server. After installing ADFS 2.0, you will open the ADFS 2.0 Management Console. The first time you open the console, you will be presented with the Overview page, as seen in Fig. 4.1. The Overview page gives you the option to run the ADFS 2.0 Federation Server Configuration Wizard. The wizard will guide you through the steps needed to configure your federation server.

The first screen of the wizard is the welcome screen as seen in Fig. 4.2. Here you choose whether the server you are configuring will be a part of a new Federation Service or if it will be added to an existing Federation Service. If this server is the first federation server in your ADFS implementation, choose "Create a new Federation Service." If you choose "Add a federation server to an existing Federation Service," you will be prompted to enter the name of the primary federation server of the Federation Service instance.

An instance of ADFS is sometimes called a Federation Service.

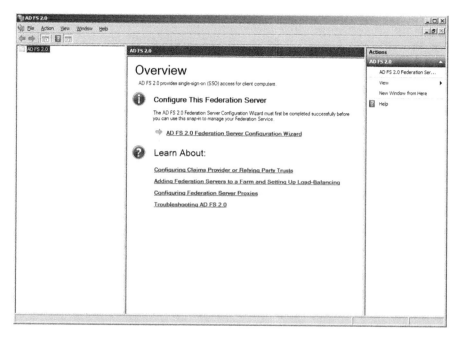

Fig. 4.1. ADFS Management Console Overview page.

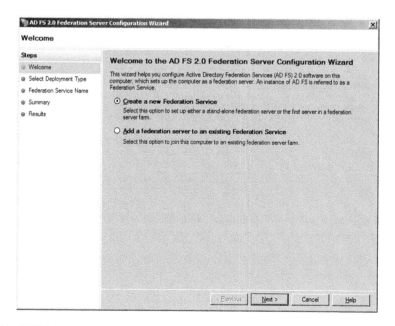

Fig. 4.2. ADFS Federation Server Configuration Wizard welcome screen.

The next screen you will see is the Deployment Type screen, as seen in Fig. 4.3. If you chose to create a new Federation Service, here you will have the option to either create a *New federation server farm* or to create a *Standalone federation server*. If you create a federation server farm, you can later add more federation servers to your farm to provide load balancing and high availability. If you choose to create a standalone federation server, these options will not be available to you. This section of the book assumes that you choose to create a new federation server farm.

The next screen is the Federation Service Name screen (Fig. 4.4). The wizard will query the server's Default Web Site for an appropriate certificate. The wizard will then pull the Subject name from the certificate. The wizard will show that name as the Federation Service Name.

The next screen is the Service Account screen, as seen in Fig. 4.5. Here you must specify a service account to be used to manage your server farm. The account you use for the service account must have access to all of the servers in the farm. It must also have rights to create a container in Active Directory.

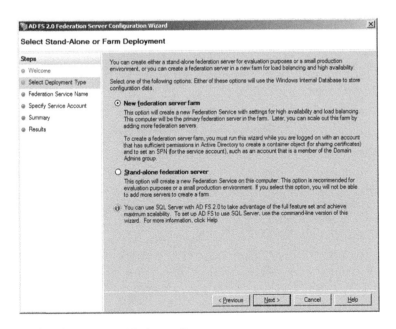

Fig. 4.3. ADFS Configuration Wizard Deployment Type screen.

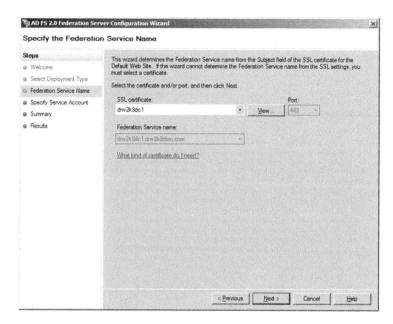

Fig. 4.4. ADFS Configuration Wizard Federation Service Name screen.

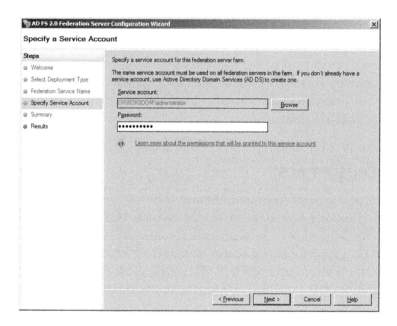

Fig. 4.5. ADFS Config Wizard Service Account screen.

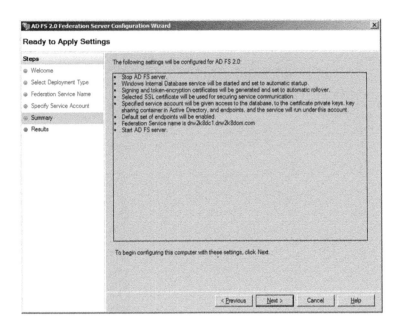

Fig. 4.6. ADFS Config Wizard Summary screen.

Next, you will be presented with the Summary screen, as seen in Fig. 4.6. The Summary screen tells you what actions are about to take place.

Finally, the Results screen as seen in Fig. 4.7 will let you know if everything was successful or not. You should review any errors or warnings that are presented.

4.4 MICROSOFT ACS

When choosing your federated identity solution, you can choose to go with an externally hosted issuer like Microsoft ACS. ACS is a Window Azure cloud-based web service used for identity and access management. ACS can provide authentication and authorization functionality for web applications and services. This way, those functions don't have to be built directly into the code for the application or service.

Since ACS is a cloud-based instance, there is no installation required in order to use the service. You do however have to configure ACS to properly integrate with your environment. This configuration is essential. Although ACS is externally hosted, it is not

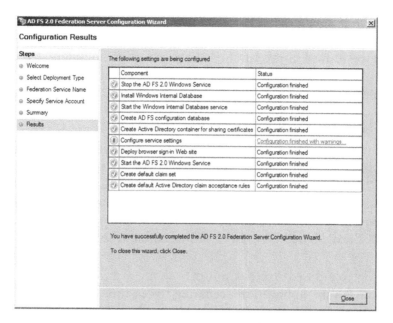

Fig. 4.7. ADFS Config Wizard Results screen.

externally managed. The service provider, in this case Microsoft, will not manage your ACS instance for you. You are responsible for doing that yourself. Microsoft will handle software upgrades and system maintenance, but they will not configure ACS for you.

ACS is very extensible. It is compliant with a large number of environments and protocols. This allows you to easily integrate ACS into your environment. ACS supports industry standard protocols like OAuth, OpenID, WS-Federation, and WS-Trust. ACS also supports multiple token formats. It supports SAML 1.2, SAML 2.0, JSON Web Tokens (JWT), and Simple Web Tokens (SWT) formats. ACS supports development using a variety of web platforms. You can use .NET, PHP, Java, Python, and a host of others.

4.4.1 ACS Functionality

ACS includes a complete set of functionality critical for most federated identity environments. ACS allows you to implement only the functionality you need for your implementation. ACS provides the following functionality: Authentication, Authorization, Federation, Security Token Flow and Transformation, Trust Management, Administration, and Automation.

4.4.1.1 Authentication
ACS will perform authentication for your application. This authentication is performed using an IdP that you must configure. ACS has built-in support for a number of IdPs. It also allows you to configure integration with a custom built IdP.

4.4.1.2 Authorization
When using ACS, ACS is responsible for supplying the information that will be used to make authorization decision. ACS creates the token that will contain this information. It will then be passed to the application. The application itself will then make the authorization decisions. There are two main authorization methods that can be used with ACS: role-based access and claims-based access.

4.4.1.2.1 Role-Based Access Control
In claims-aware application scenarios, roles are expressed using the role claim type. The role claim type is expressed using the following URI: http://schemas.microsoft.com/ws/2008/06/identity/claims/role.

There are three ways to provide a role claim: use the ACS rule engine, transform a claim, or map a claim. Transforming a claim is done by using the Claims Authentication Manager. It will intercept a token, change a claim, and then pass the token along. Mapping a claim is more straightforward. It is done through the ACS configuration.

4.4.1.2.2 Claims-Based Access Control
Claims-based access control allows you to use more than just the role claim to make authorization decisions. With claims-based access control, the claims will be extracted from the application. The application will send the claims to a decision engine. This decision engine will then make the authorization decisions and send the information back to the application.

4.4.1.3 Federation
ACS integrates with a host of different IdPs including ADFS 2.0, Windows Live, Google, Yahoo, and Facebook. You can configure a federated trust with these IdPs so they can be used in your implementation. This can help keep you from having to manage users and user IDs yourself. You can allow the external IdP to take care of that.

4.4.1.4 Security Token Flow and Transformation

ACS will control the flow and processing of tokens. This is mainly done through the use of rules and rule groups. Rules determine how a token will be processed and what claims will be used. Rules can also be used to do token transformations. You can specify what the input and output claims will be. This is helpful when using an external IdP that might issue claims similar to, but different than the ones you need for your relying parties.

4.4.1.5 Trust Management

Trusts are necessary to establish a relationship between ACS and the relying party. Without a trust, ACS and the relying party will not send information back and forth. If a trust has not been established, it is very difficult to determine if any information has been tampered with during transit. Trusts are established by signing the tokens that are sent between ACS and the relying party. You can sign tokens using either x.509 certificates or symmetric keys. To create and manage the trust relationship, use the ACS Management Portal.

4.4.1.6 Administration

You administer your ACS environment using either the ACS Management Portal or the ACS Management Service. The ACS Management Portal is the simplest and most commonly used method. It's a web-based console that provides access to most ACS features and functionality. The ACS Management Service is a scriptable interface that can be used to manage ACS. The ACS Management Service is what you would use for automation. Automation will come in handy for doing repetitive tasks like adding users. In addition, the ACS Management Service provides access to some functionality not available in the ACS Management Portal.

4.4.1.7 Automation

ACS allows for automation of configuration and management. ACS comes with an OData compliant interface that can used for program-matic manipulation of your ACS instance. This automation is done using the ACS Management Service.

4.4.2 ACS Components

An ACS architecture consists of the following components: the ACS namespace, IdPs, relying party application, rules and rule groups, service identities, certificates and keys, the management portal, the management service, and Login Pages and Home Realm Discovery.

4.4.2.1 Service Namespace
The ACS namespace is the logical entity that represents an ACS implementation. The namespace is also the administrative boundary, meaning all your configuration for an ACS instance is done for a particular namespace. All of your ACS components and services are based on your namespace. Most of these components and services are accessed via a URI subdomain using your namespace. Your namespace will use four endpoints representing the STS (Secure Token Service), the Management Service, the Management Portal, and Service Metadata.

4.4.2.2 Identity Providers
ACS allows you to configure external IdPs for authentication. These IdPs will authenticate the user and issue a token. ACS will take the claims in the token and use them to create a token that will be accepted by its relying parties. There are two ways to configure IdPs in ACS: either through the Management Portal or using the Management Service. Either method will allow you to configure trusts with Windows Live ID, Yahoo, Google, Facebook, and WS-Federation providers. In addition, the Management Service will also allow you to configure trusts with OpenID and WS-Trust providers.

4.4.2.3 Relying Party
Relying party applications are the applications and services that will be serviced by ACS. An explicit trust is configured between your ACS namespace and each relying party ACS will service. ACS allows you to configure the following properties for your relying parties: mode, realm and return URL, error URL, token format, token encryption policy, token lifetime, IdPs, rule groups, token signing, and token encryption.

4.4.2.4 Rules and Rule Groups
A rule group is used to define a set of claims that will be passed from an IdP to a relying party. A rule group can be used by multiple relying parties. A single relying party can also reference multiple rule groups. When ACS receives a token request or a token from an IdP, it will go through all the rule groups associated with the relying party. It will then process the appropriate claims in the token. Rules and rule groups

are created and/or edited using the ACS Management Portal or the ACS Management Service.

All rule groups and all rules within a group are processed simultaneously; therefore, the order in which rules and rule groups are entered does not matter.

Claim rules define how token transformations are done. ACS will receive a token from an IdP. Based on the rules that are configured, ACS will create a new token that will be used by the relying party. The power of this feature comes from the fact that the new output claims don't have to have to be related to the input claims. You can use a completely different set of claims as your output claims.

4.4.2.5 Service Identities
A service identity is a credential registered with an ACS namespace. They are used by autonomous applications and clients. A service identity allows an application or client to authenticate directly with ACS. Service Identities can use symmetric keys, passwords, or x.509 certificates for authentication.

Use caution when configuring service identities. Passwords used with service identities are sent in plain text, so encrypting the stream itself is very important.

4.4.2.6 Certificates and Keys
ACS allows you to configure signing and encryption for different token types. You can sign, encrypt, and decrypt SAML tokens using x.509 certificates. You can use asymmetric keys to sign SWT token. This is all done using the ACS Management Portal or through the ACS Management Service.

4.4.2.7 ACS Management Portal
The ACS Management Portal is launched through the Windows Azure Management Portal. The ACS Management Portal is used to configure most aspects of your ACS environment. The portal allows you to configure IdPs, relying parties, rule groups and rules, certificates and keys, service identities, portal administrators, and the ACS Management Service. Most of these components are covered in other

sections. The exception is portal administrators. So we will cover them a little bit here.

When you create your ACS namespace, it is created with only one administrator account. This is the account that was used to create the namespace. The portal administrator section of the ACS Management Portal allows you to grant administrative access to a designated namespace within ACS to users from a particular IdP.

4.4.2.8 ACS Management Service

The ACS Management Service allows you automate certain aspects of ACS configuration and management. The ACS Management Service can be accessed using the OData (Open Data Protocol). This allows you to programmatically manage your ACS configuration. The ACS namespace contains default data that is not available to the Management Portal, but it is available to the ACS Management Service. This data includes the following: AccessControlManagement Relying Party Application, AccessControlManagement Rule Group and Rules, Windows Live ID IdP and Issuer, and LOCAL_AUTHORITY Issuer.

To access the ACS Management Service, you need to use an OData client. You will need to point the client to the ACS Management Service endpoint URL. Before configuration can begin, the client must be authenticated. This is done through the use of an ACS Management Service account. The service account can be authenticated using username and password, symmetric keys, or x.509 certificates.

OData, the Open Data Protocol, is used for querying and updating data. OData was originally developed by Microsoft as a REST-based protocol to provide CRUD (Create, Read, Update, and Delete) access to data services. You can think of it as a web-based equivalent of Open Database Connectivity (ODBC).

4.4.2.9 Login Pages and Home Realm Discovery

There are two ways authentication can be configured in ACS. You can configure ACS to provide the login page or you can configure ACS so that your application provides a custom login page.

ACS will provide a very basic login page. The login page is hosted by ACS at the WS-Federation protocol endpoint for your namespace.

If you want to change the login page, then you need to use a custom login page hosted by your application. If you want, you can simply copy the default login page from ACS to your application. There you will be able to customize it.

The default login page will include the Home Realm Discovery Metadata Feed. This feed is what is used to connect to the IdP. This makes it a little easier to ensure your changes to the web page don't affect the actual authentication process. As long as this feed is not modified, you shouldn't have a problem. Or if you create a page scratch, as long the page can communicate with JSON, it should be able to communicate with the feed.

4.4.3 Using ACS
The most common method for configuring ACS is through the ACS Management Portal. In this section, we will go through a brief over-view of what can be done through the portal. When you access the ACS Management Portal, one of the first things you should take note of is that at the top of the portal, you can see the namespace that your ACS instance is managing. You will also note that the ACS Administration Portal has five headings: Home, Trust relationships, Service settings, Administration, and Development.

4.4.3.1 Home
The Home section contains the ACS Administration Portal Home Page. The Home Section of the ACS Administration portal, as seen in Fig. 4.8, contains a Getting Started section that gives you basic infor-mation about what's need to get your ACS implementation going. The first area of the Getting Started sections gives you the option to per-form the steps needed to configure single sign-on to a web application. These steps include adding IdPs, adding relying parties, creating rule groups, and integrating ACS authentication code with your applica-tion. The second area provides you with information about configuring authentication and authorization for web applications and web services.

4.4.3.2 Trust Relationships
The Trust relationships section allows you to establish the various trusts that are needed in an ACS implementation. You also configure rules around how the entity on one side of trust handles interaction with the entity on the other side of the trust. The Trust

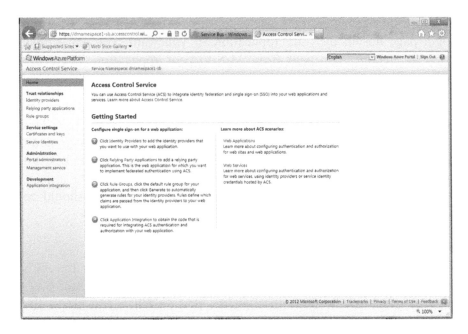

Fig. 4.8. Access Control Service Administration Portal Home Page.

relationships heading includes three sections: IdPs, Relying party applications, and rule groups.

4.4.3.2.1 Identity Providers

As seen in Fig. 4.9, the IdPs section will display all the IdPs that you have configured with your ACS instance. You also use this section to add IdPs to or remove them from your ACS instance. The default IdP is the one you use to log in to your ACS instance.

To add another IdP, click the Add link. The Add Identity Provider page seen in Fig. 4.10 will appear. Here you have the option to choose which IdP you would like to add. Your options are a WS-Federation provider, a Facebook application, Google, and Yahoo.

4.4.3.2.2 Relying Party Applications

As seen in Fig. 4.11, the Relying party applications section will display all the relying parties that trust your ACS implementation. Relying parties can be web applications, web sites, or web services. This section also allows you to add or delete a relying party.

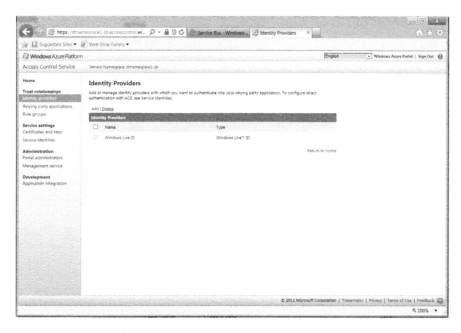

Fig. 4.9. ACS Admin Console Identity Providers screen

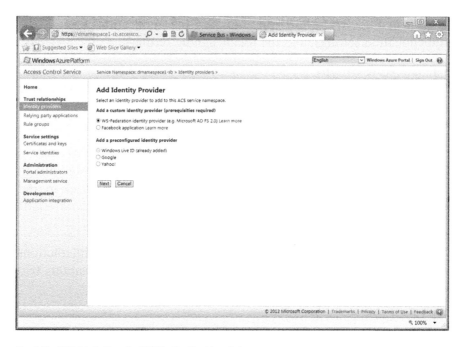

Fig. 4.10. ACS Admin Console Add Identity Provider window.

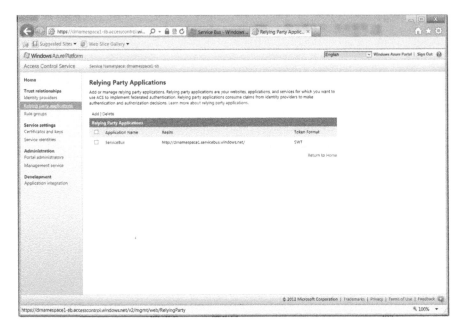

Fig. 4.11. ACS Admin Console Relying Party applications section.

Clicking Add will bring up the Add Relying Party Application page as seen in Fig. 4.12. Here you configure the application settings, the authentication settings, and the token signing settings.

4.4.3.2.3 Rule Groups
As seen in Fig. 4.13, the Rule Groups section allows you to view rule groups that have been configured for your instance. You can also add new rule groups and delete existing ones.

Selecting Add will bring up the Add Rule Group page as seen in Fig. 4.14. Here you enter the name of the rule group you would like to create. After the rule group has been created, you can go back in and configure the rules for that group.

4.4.3.3 Service Settings
The Service settings section is used to configure service interactions within your ACS instance. The Service settings heading contains two sections: Certificates and Keys and Service Identities.

4.4.3.3.1 Certificates and Keys
As seen in Fig. 4.15, the Certificates and Keys section allows you to configure token signing keys and token encryption keys.

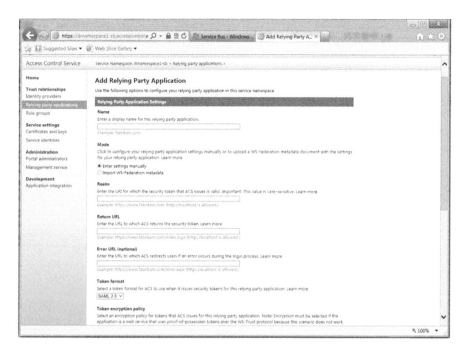

Fig. 4.12. ACS Admin Console Add Relying Party Application window.

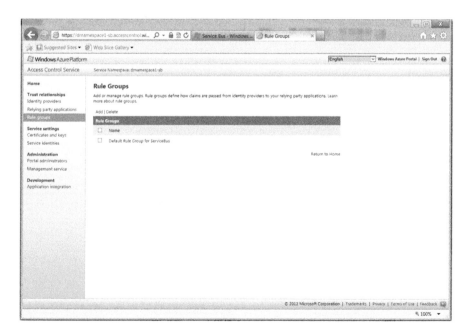

Fig. 4.13. ACS Admin Console Rule Groups section.

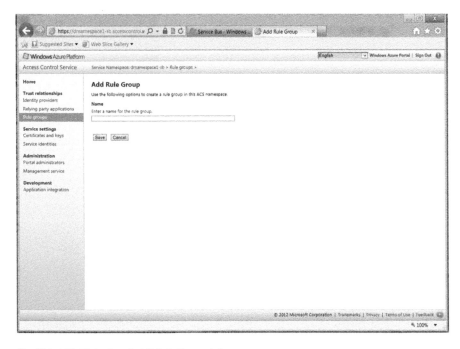

Fig. 4.14. ACS Admin Console Add Rule Group window.

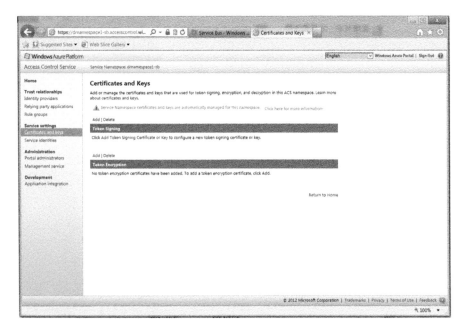

Fig. 4.15. ACS Admin Console Certificates and Keys section.

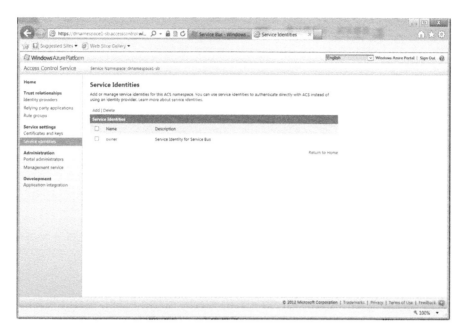

Fig. 4.16. ACS Admin Portal Service Identities section.

4.4.3.3.2 Service Identities

As seen in Fig. 4.16, the Service Identities section lists out the service identities configured for your instance. Service identities are used to authenticate directly against ACS. No IdP is needed.

Clicking Add will bring up the Add Service Identities page as seen in Fig. 4.17. Here you configure your service identity settings and the associated credential settings.

4.4.3.4 Administration

You use the Administration section to configure the administrative functions of your ACS instance. There are two sections available here: Portal administrators and Management service.

4.4.3.4.1 Portal Administrators

As seen in Fig. 4.18, the Portal administrators shows you the users that currently have administrative access to the ACS instance and the URL that these administrators can use to access the ACS Administration Portal.

Clicking Add will bring up the Add Portal Administrator page, as seen in Fig. 4.19. On the Add Portal Administrator screen, you must

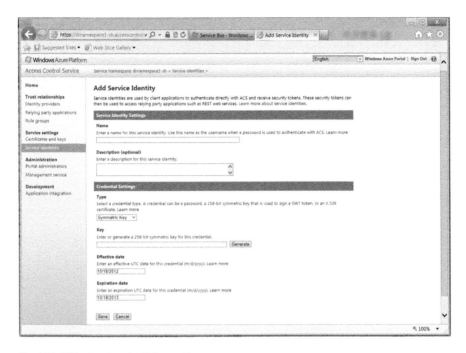

Fig. 4.17. ACS Admin Portal Add Service Identity page.

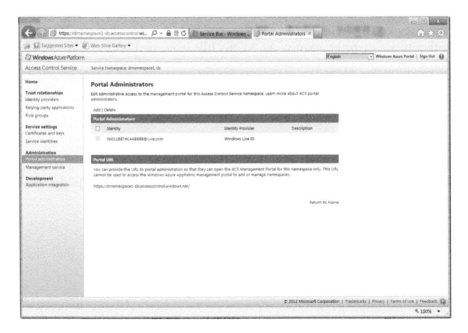

Fig. 4.18. ACS Portal Administrators section.

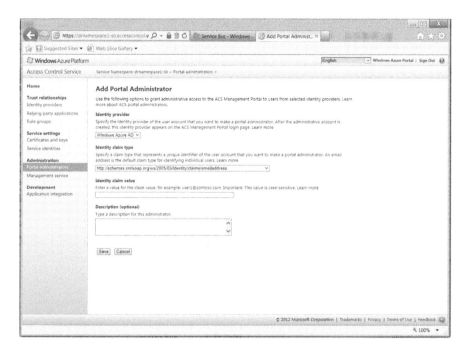

Fig. 4.19. ACS Add Portal Administrators screen.

enter the IdP used to authenticate the user, the claim type and value used to identify the user, and an optional description.

Administrators can use the URL shown under Portal URL to gain direct access to the ACS Admin Portal for this instance. They do not have to go through the Windows Azure Admin Portal.

4.4.3.4.2 Management Service

As seen in Fig. 4.20, the Management Service section provides two functions. You can manage Management Service accounts here. You can also view the Management Service URL that would be needed by your OData client. This is the URL the client would need to use in order to be able to manage your ACS instance.

If you click Add, you will be able to add a new Management Service account. As seen in Fig. 4.21, on the Add Management Service Account page, you will need to configure your service account settings and the credential settings.

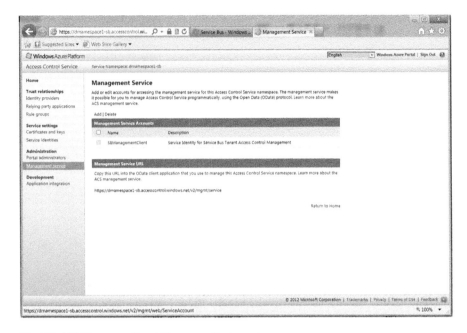

Fig. 4.20. ACS Management Portal Management Service section.

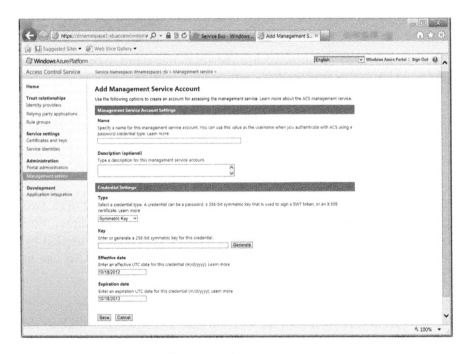

Fig. 4.21. ACS Management Portal Add Management Service Account page.

4.4.3.5 Development

Your federated identity solution will probably require some level of development. The Development section is where you configure development-related settings and access information on how to develop against your ACS implementation. The Development heading contains only one section called Application Integration.

4.4.3.5.1 Application Integration

As seen in Fig. 4.22, you can use the Application Integration section to guide you in integrating ACS with your applications. You integrate ACS into your login page, view ACS documentation, access ACS Software Development Kits (SDKs), and view a list of the endpoints associated with your ACS instance.

Clicking Login Pages will bring up the Login Page Integration page as seen in Fig. 4.23. On the Login Page Integration page, you select the relying party application that you want to configure. ACS will then provide you with the information that you need to configure the login page for this application.

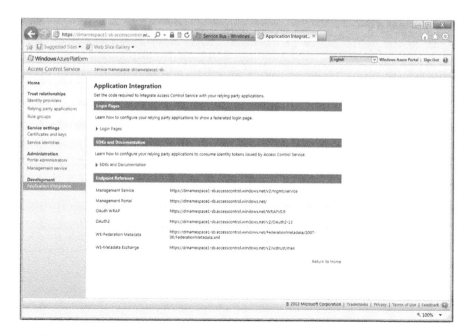

Fig. 4.22. ACS Admin Portal Application Integration section.

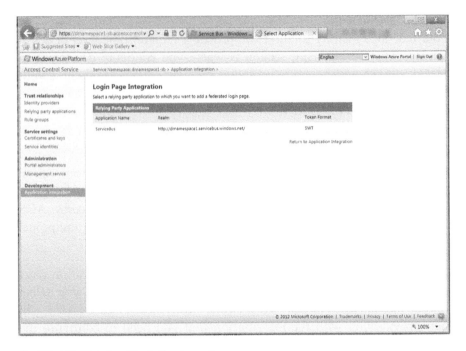

Fig. 4.23. ACS Admin Portal Login Page Integration page.

4.5 SUMMARY

Choosing which federated identity solution to implement can be a complex decision. Each solution is different, and making the right decision for organization requires careful attention. You have to consider a lot of factors, including cost, interoperability, and security. You can choose an internal solution or an external solution; an out-of-the-box solution or a custom-built solution. Microsoft ADFS 2.0 and Microsoft ACS are two of the more widely used solutions. ADFS 2.0 is generally installed internally to your organization. ACS is a hosted solution built on top of the Microsoft Azure platform.